Advance Praise for
The Heart of Hospitality

"Sooner or later, we're all in the hospitality business. I bet you'll find that chapter 8 alone is worth the cost of the book."

—**Seth Godin**
Author of *What to Do When It's Your Turn*

"At Virgin Hotels, we are building a new hotel experience–something that can only be done by learning lessons from the greats of our industry and understanding the needs and wants of today's consumers. In *The Heart of Hospitality*, Micah Solomon—one of the true thought leaders of the customer experience—has gathered unparalleled hospitality wisdom and distilled it in an incredibly readable and useful format. We were delighted to be part of this project and recommend it to any company or individual looking to grow within our industry."

—**Raul Leal**
CEO, Virgin Hotels

"A spectacularly useful, intelligent, and wry look at what determines success in the hospitality industry."

—**Herve Humler**
President and COO, The Ritz Carlton Hotel Company

"In this groundbreaking new book, Micah Solomon manages to distill the wisdom of some of America's most enlightened hospitality professionals. He combines the power of their insights with his own refreshing point of view in a compelling narrative style that is concise and to the point. *The Heart of Hospitality* illustrates that ultimately it is the human connection that builds and sustains guest loyalty. This is an inspirational and useful book for anyone interested in customer satisfaction. Is there anyone who isn't?"

—**Patrick O'Connell**
Chef/Proprietor, The Inn at Little Washington

"An incredibly valuable look at the hospitality industry, hospitality management, and how to succeed with today's (and tomorrow's) guests."

—**Sara Kearney**
Vice President, Hyatt Hotels Corporation

"It's ironic, but many people and organizations in our industry fail because they lack knowledge and insight for how to provide true hospitality, how to truly care for the guest. That's why *The Heart of Hospitality* is so important. It steps in to fill this gap. And it fills it with knowledge from the very best: hospitality icons Isadore Sharp, founder and chairman of Four Seasons Hotels and Resorts; Herve Humler, president and COO of The Ritz-Carlton Hotel Company; Danny Meyer, president and CEO of Union Square Hospitality Group, and so many more. Micah Solomon has interviewed the key executives from hospitality's best, including those from The Broadmoor and The Inn at Little Washington, Montage, Fairmont, EDITION, and Virgin Hotels and has merged their insights with his own as one of the best and best-known customer service experts himself.

Their collective insight focuses on all the key ingredients to deliver an exceptional guest experience—hiring the right people, developing the necessary internal systems and hospitality standards, creating the proper service culture, defining steps for service recovery and visualizing anticipatory service, as well as offering fascinating and essential discussions on how technology has and will change the guest experience.

—**Bill Quiseng**
Hospitality-industry GM
(Radisson, Renaissance, Autograph Collection)

"Micah Solomon has gathered all of the great hospitality industry heroes, hotel management practitioners and great restaurateurs together and pulled crucial hospitality management and business insights out of them. This is transformational to the reader who wants to thrive in the challenging world of hospitality and hospitality management."

—**Rupesh Patel**
President and CEO, 3Hospitality

THE **HEART** OF **HOSPITALITY**

THE HEART OF HOSPITALITY

Great Hotel and Restaurant Leaders Share Their Secrets

MICAH SOLOMON

SelectBooks, Inc.
New York

This edition published by SelectBooks, Inc.
For information address SelectBooks, Inc., New York, New York.

First Edition

ISBN 978-1-59079-378-7

Library of Congress Cataloging-in-Publication Data

Names: Solomon, Micah, author.
Title: The heart of hospitality : great hotel and restaurant leaders share
  their secrets / Micah Solomon.
Description: First edition. | New York : SelectBooks, Inc., [2016] |
Includes
  bibliographical references and index. | Includes bibliographical
  references and index.
Identifiers: LCCN 2015040050 | ISBN 9781590793787 (hardcover book : alk.
  paper)
Subjects: LCSH: Hospitality industry--Management. | Food service management.
Classification: LCC TX911.3.M27 S684 2016 | DDC 647.95068--dc23 LC record
available at http://lccn.loc.gov/2015040050

The publisher and the author provide this material on the condition that the reader understand that we are not in the business of providing legal, accounting, or safety-related practice
advice, or any other professional advice, and that all information herein is intended for general
consideration rather than as necessarily applicable to any particular situation of the reader.

Book design by Janice Benight

Manufactured in the United States of America
10 9 8 7 6 5 4 3 2 1

dedicate *The Heart of Hospitality* to my family, who were generous and patient about the many hours I spent writing and traveling in order to create this book, and encouraged and assisted me with this all-consuming endeavor.

And I dedicate it to the hospitality professionals who contributed their unique voices and insights to this project: Herve Humler and the entire Ritz-Carlton organization (with very special thanks to Allison Sitch); Tom Colicchio of Crafted Hospitality; Danny Meyer and his Union Square Hospitality Group; Isadore Sharp, Christopher Hunsberger, and Andreas Rippel at Four Seasons Hotels and Resorts; Patrick O'Connell at The Inn at Little Washington; Steve Bartolin and Ann Alba at The Broadmoor; Mark Harmon at Auberge Resorts; Jazz Buchla and Seth McDaniels at Joie de Vivre Hotels; Jennifer Fox, Doug Carr, and Shelley Meszoly at FRHI (Fairmont-Raffles-Swissotel); Jay Coldren at Marriott; Mark Hoplamazian and Sara Kearney at Hyatt; Raul Leal and Clio Knowles at Virgin Hotels; Robin, Curt, and Kim Baney at Oxford Suites; Craig Schoninger and Christine Wrobel at Montage Resorts; hospitality thought leaders Bill Quiseng and Tim Miller; Raj Singh at Go Moment; Brad Black at HUMANeX; Rupesh Patel at 3Hospitality and SmartGuests.com; John Meadow at LDV Hospitality; Garrett Harker at Eastern Standard Kitchen & Drinks; Jim Reid-Anderson, Nancy Kresja, John Bement, Jayson Maxwell, and Richard Payson at Six Flags Entertainment Corp.; Glenn Lawless at Mohegan Sun Pocono; Leo Fenn III at Selanne Steak Tavern, Bob Johnston of Front Burner Brands; David Rockwell at The Rockwell Group; Laura Romanoff at The Maya Romanoff Company; Fred Dust at IDEO; Suzy Hankins at The Ant Street Inn; Diane MacPherson at The Foster Harris House; Stephen Starr at STARR Restaurants, Traci Des Jardins of Jardinière et al., and Eric Ripert at Les Bernardin.

CONTENTS

Foreword

There have been volumes written—complete curricula, in fact—that cover the technical, nuts-and-bolts, RevPAR [revenue per available room] side of the hospitality industry. But what about the soul, the heart of what makes great hospitality? How do you create (and sustain) a level of service so memorable that it becomes a defining part of your brand and an unbeatable competitive advantage?

You'll find many of the answers in the book you now hold in your hands, *The Heart of Hospitality*. Micah Solomon has put together the only book of its kind: a spectacularly useful, intelligent, and wry look at what determines success in the hospitality industry, packing it throughout with his own insights and the insights of an extraordinary roster of great leaders and practitioners from our industry today.

Micah is one of today's preeminent thought leaders on where hospitality, customer service, and customers themselves are heading. As an avid reader of his earlier works, I was honored by the invitation to help bring this volume to life with access to our General Managers, the Ladies and Gentlemen who helm our Leadership Center, our technology initiatives, our branding and marketing efforts, and behind-the-scenes looks at the practices that make our Ritz-Carlton hotels and resorts premier destinations.

The other industry leaders who have contributed their perspectives to *The Heart of Hospitality* notably include, in lodging, Steve Bartolin at The Broadmoor Hotel, Isadore Sharp at Four Seasons Hotels and Resorts, Mark Harmon at Auberge Resorts, Raul Leal at Virgin Hotels, Mark Hoplamazian and his Hyatt brands, Jennifer Fox at Fairmont, and more. On the culinary side of the equation, you will find insights from notable restaurateurs and others in the world of F&B [food and beverage], including Danny Meyer, Eric Ripert, Tom Colicchio, Patrick O'Connell, Traci Des Jardins, Stephen Starr, and others.

Our industry is both timeless and evolving very rapidly. To achieve and sustain success in hospitality, we must keep pace with changing guests and their changing expectations. Micah explains (at length in chapter 9 as well as throughout the book) what's involved in making the changes that are necessary to keep up. His predictions and research about how travelers—travelers of all ages and millennials in particular—are changing the world of hospitality are absolutely spot-on and are important to take to heart.

My greatest joy and thrill in life is helping others succeed. I truly believe that *The Heart of Hospitality* will be instrumental in boosting your outcomes in our exciting industry. Wherever you are in your journey within the hospitality industry, the insights and lessons inside are essential.

Read it, earmark it, highlight it, *learn it.*

You will be well served.

—HERVE HUMLER
President and COO
The Ritz-Carlton Hotel Company, LLC

Introduction

Steve Jobs was determined (as only Steve could be) to build a customer service experience at the Apple Stores that would rival the best customer service to be found anywhere, in any industry. So, before opening a single Apple Store to the public, he made his rounds among the employees at Apple headquarters in Cupertino, asking a single question, over and over: "What's the best experience you've ever had as a customer?" Nearly every answer he got back, from nearly every employee, was similar, and, no, they weren't tales of superlative experiences as customers at CompUSA (RIP), Circuit City (ditto), or any of the other electronics retailers against which the Apple Stores would soon be competing.

The answer Steve kept hearing from his Apple employees was that the best customer experiences in the world were taking place at Ritz-Carlton hotels, Four Seasons resorts, and other exemplars of the hospitality industry. These responses convinced Jobs to insist that those involved in the creation of the Apple Stores study, benchmark, and emulate the hospitality industry. The impact of this decision is most visible in Apple Stores' "Genius Bar" (a direct tribute to a hotel concierge area) but goes much deeper, affecting everything from Apple Store hiring practices to how employees greet customers and bid them farewell.

Steve Jobs' admiration for the hospitality industry was right on target. There truly is no other type of business that is better at transforming the essentials of everyday life—a room, a bed, a sink, a toilet, a meal—into an experience that is warm, comforting, memorable, and perhaps even magical.

The opportunity you'll find within these pages is the chance to learn how this hospitality industry magic is created and sustained. You'll learn directly from the very best in the business: the CEOs, GMs, chefs, and other visionaries at the greatest hospitality companies in the world. I've packed the pages of this book with their perspectives on the culture, hiring, training, systems, and philosophical framework necessary to bring extraordinary hospitality to life, day after day and night after night in the face of changing customer fashions and expectations.

This is important, powerful stuff. It's drawn from exclusive interviews I've made over the course of many months specifically for this book. (At the end of this book, you'll find a listing of everyone who contributed the interviews on which this book is based.) I also made site visits to many of the great and innovative hotels, resorts, and restaurants in the industry. I've shaped and rounded out this material based on my own insights as a consultant, speaker, and business leader working both inside and outside the hospitality industry. And I've closed out every chapter with a summary titled **"And Your Point Is?"** It's filled with key points in an abbreviated format that's intended to serve a similar purpose as the Cliffs Notes® some of us depended on in school.

So, I hope you enjoy learning from the best of the best—the greatest leaders and professionals at the best lodging and food service organizations in the world.

◆ ◆ ◆

A bit about me: I work across a wide range of industries as a customer service consultant, keynote speaker, and trainer. I have a long background in assisting companies to become successful by creating and maintaining superior customer service and an exemplary customer experience. (If you'd like the examples or lessons in this book to be made specific to you or your organization, please let me know by emailing me at micah@ micahsolomon.com or calling me directly at (484)343-5881. In keeping with a customer service best practice, I answer my own phone.)

Notes to the reader about the content of *The Heart of Hospitality*:

Portions of this material have appeared, in the same or a more preliminary form, in the author's online articles and short-form eBooks.

In some inevitable cases, employee titles and employment status will have changed between the time of an interview and the date of publication. In these cases, the title and employment status as of the time of the interview have been retained in the text.

THE **HEART** OF
HOSPITALITY

1

The Last Customer on Earth

"The only metric a guest cares about is this: one to one.
That one guest in front of one associate. Will that associate take care
of me? And **does** that associate care about me?"*
—Hospitality professional BILL QUISENG

Out of nowhere, a dog bounds up to the reception desk of the Hyatt House hotel in suburban Virginia, clearly on a mission. The front desk agent leans over and tosses a rolled newspaper into the dog's waiting mouth. With this stage of his mission accomplished, the dog walks away with his tail wagging, and the agent goes back to work processing paperwork for the next guest.

A Colleague and a Collie

Has Hyatt House resorted to employing bell staff of the four-legged variety? Actually, this dog is a guest of sorts. "His owner had just sold her home after 40 years of living there and, like many of our guests at Hyatt House, is in a bit of limbo before moving into her first apartment space as an empty-nester," explains Hyatt senior vice president Sara Kearney. "My colleague at the front desk [at this point in the interview I had to confirm that Kearney had said "colleague," not "collie"] has been trying to help

---

* All quotations in this book, including this one, are taken from interviews conducted for this book by Micah Solomon, unless indicated otherwise. A complete list of those who contributed interviews is on page 197.

this guest maintain some semblance of her routine from her previous life. So each morning her dog pads down the hall to the front desk, gets the newspaper just like he did when they lived at home, and carries it back to the guest room where his master awaits."

Hospitality guests are by definition dislocated. They're not eating at home, not sleeping at home—they're *away*. Though this displacement is no doubt voluntary at a resort location or a trip to a restaurant, at an extended-stay property like Hyatt House (the economically priced, extended-stay hotel brand that Hyatt carved out of its AmeriSuites acquisition), the dislocation is likely to be the result of an awkward and possibly painful situation. Guests here include the recently divorced, those enduring job assignments away from their families, and those whose houses have sold before they've settled on a new one. These are situations where the psychological realities of a guest's life can be weighing heavily on their perception of the goods and services you're providing. And it's a situation where true service—hospitality—can shine.

But it can't shine when delivered in an assembly-line fashion. It needs to be focused on one guest at a time. What Hyatt House was doing for this guest was specific to her, and, therefore, meaningful.

That's the crux of the matter—the opportunity and challenge that we'll be exploring in this chapter. Treating a guest as your *only* guest, focusing on what your guest needs beyond a secure lock on the door, an appropriate room rate, a meal *sans* salmonella, and so forth, is where you'll find the opportunity to distinguish yourself in hospitality—to build an advantage that competitors will find harder to knock off than the momentary advantages of perks like two-for-one desserts.

It's All About That Focus

Let's leave Hyatt House and travel to what's considered one of the most extraordinary restaurants and small hotels in the United States. We'll still be in Virginia, but are otherwise far afield. We're going to have dinner at

Patrick O'Connell's legendary restaurant called The Inn at Little Washington, a double Five Star (per Forbes), double Five Diamond (per AAA) restaurant and inn in the rural county of Rappahannock, home to only 7,000 full-time human residents as well as a significant number of sheep, cattle, and, for some obscure reason, ostriches.

In addition to all the other superlatives that have been voiced about The Inn at Little Washington ("Best Restaurant in America," "Most Beautiful Kitchen in the World," and on and on), here's one more that fits: "Situated in the ultimate of inconvenient locations." One time, in fact, a friend of mine who was peeved at me for picking such an out-of-the-way location for our get-together, crankily described the route he was required to travel. He said, "*First,* I had to drive to the middle of nowhere. *Then,* I had to drive *another* thirty minutes to get here."

Yet food- and experience-obsessed guests have made this beautiful and inconvenient spot a pilgrimage site. Guests have included kings, queens, and presidents (actual presidents and those of the mere popularly-elected variety—Al Gore and then-wife Tipper had their anniversary dinner at The Inn every year) as well as true gourmets without rank or status have saved their money for months, years, or a decade to be able to experience the food and hospitality of the inn for a night.

Of course, there are a lot of different pieces that go into creating the double Five Star (twenty-four years straight with the Forbes/Mobil Travel Guide) double Five Diamond (twenty-five years straight with AAA) gem that is The Inn at Little Washington: The kitchen. The training. The décor by London stage designer Joyce Evans. Exclusive farm and sourcing resources. The gentle comedy of Faira, the cow on wheels that brings the cheese course around the dining room, her tableside arrival announced by the ringing tones of her cowbell. And, of course, Chef O'Connell himself, famously dubbed "the Pope of American Cuisine" by the late, leading vineyard operator Robert Mondavi. But the one facet that O'Connell tells me has to shine beyond all others to make the entire operation succeed is *focus*—a complete focus on the guest, one person at a time.

The heart of hospitality, for me, is the ability to focus completely and totally on one person, even if only for a matter of seconds, yet long enough that you've got a clear connection, a channel between the two of you. It's the ability to focus so intently on a guest that the rest of the world ceases to exist. It might sound, as I tell you this, that this type of focus takes a lot of time, but it doesn't; it just requires your full and complete attention at a given moment. You have to develop the discipline of momentarily blotting out the rest of the world. Believe me: your guest will know immediately when you've succeeded.

As an antecedent to his approach, O'Connell gives a nod to "the geishas in Japan who can make a patron feel, for the time they are together, like the most important person in the world. In today's world, if you think about it, we're often so fractured and distracted that we barely even make eye contact with people. Now, if you have a *puppy*, everybody's going to make eye contact with the little puppy and light up and be intrigued, but when encountering another human being, sometimes we have a tendency, from shyness, weariness, who knows, to do the opposite and blot them out. But what could possibly be more important than the person standing in front of you?"

O'Connell offered me a recent example of his approach to connecting with guests:

A woman recently ate in our dining room by herself, reading her book through the course of the meal. I asked my staff, "Did you interact with her?" They told me, "We tried, of course, but she's somewhat reserved and hasn't given us much information to work with." Because we were at a bit of a loss for how to make a connection, at the end of the meal her waiter invited her back to the kitchen to visit with us. She came in, still carrying her book. As it turned out, I had read the same book, so I was able to make a comment or two about it. Immediately, she opened up and said that she was there celebrating her husband's birthday. He had died the year before at a very young age, and it [The Inn at Little Washington] was always a place they had planned to come together, so she was making the visit herself in his memory. I thought to myself: "Imagine if she had come all the way out here and not had an opportunity to share that information!" Being able to do so made it much more of a complete experience for her.

Customers are always giving you cues that are specific to that customer, and you have to be paying attention, every single time. Customers want you to be a "participant observer," someone who will share the experience with them. They want someone else to know the significance of the experience. They're often looking for someone with whom they can faithfully share information, and if they ever sense that you're uninterested or too busy, they won't.

Chef O'Connell has been in the business for decades—ever since 1978 when O'Connell opened his fledgling inn on the location of a former garage. Yet he and his staff still put the concept of single-guest focus into practice every day. That O'Connell has managed to *sustain* this commitment is extremely rare, as I can professionally attest.

Frequently, I'm brought in as a consultant when things are going inexplicably south at a previously thriving company in hospitality or another service-intensive field. When I start advising in this later period of stalled or negative growth, I'll pore through records and relics from the early, more auspicious days, looking for clues to what has since changed. Invariably, I'll find that in those early days, the level of detail the business kept on each customer, the number of customer follow-ups and the care taken with each one, was at a level that was impressive, even *epic*, as my kids would say.

Unfortunately, the focus and attentiveness that's common when a business has only a few customers tends to slide when those customer numbers multiply. You stop keeping, or at least stop referring back to, detailed notes on the likes and dislikes of every guest. Employees stop signing their thank-you notes by hand. Managers hide in their offices rather than coming out to greet arriving customers. The bean counters get rid of Jackie and Joanne, your quirkily charismatic veteran telephone operators whom the guests all adored, and replace them with a lower paid rookie, or even an auto-attendant "voice jail" system.

Is such slippage of standards inevitable? Not if you stick to your guns. Here's how I'd summarize the attitude of the great hoteliers, restaurateurs, and other hospitality professionals whose inspiration fills these pages: *If we did it for our first guest, we'll find a way to keep doing it for our millionth,* without rushing or cutting corners, without doing anything that would make that guest feel any less than fully valued in our eyes.

Don't Stop Believin'

The secret, in other words, is to never stop believing in the importance of the individual guest and the individual guest interaction, no matter how many guests your organization has grown to serve. Don't ever fall into the trap of thinking that there is an infinite supply of guests out there for the taking, if only your marketing and sales departments would do their jobs. The hospitality greats instead tell themselves there's just one guest, the one they're facing *right now.*

The BUBL Method

If you don't mind leaving pastoral Virginia for the glamor of Midtown Manhattan, let's head to The Ritz-Carlton New York, Central Park, specifically to the hotel's Club Level, where guests enjoy four daily food presentations and the service of a dedicated concierge and a team of attendants. I've brought you here not to enjoy the quintillion-dollar views of the park but to look at how the club environment in a great hotel offers a setting where hospitality professionals are called on to provide service in an unusually pure, distilled fashion. What the Ladies and Gentlemen (as employees proudly refer to themselves here at The Ritz-Carlton) do in a Club Level lounge is more free-form, less dependent on a specific, predictable routine than what you'll find in traditional lodging or F&B (food and beverage). Employees here aren't serving carefully timed courses that need to arrive concurrently or consecutively in correct succession. They're not checking in guests at a peak entry period. Instead, they're at their guests' service throughout the day in whatever capacity may be useful, a loosely defined role whose success hinges on whether they manage to provide that service in a way that will be appreciated, rather than coming across as an interruption.

So as I hunch over my laptop in The Ritz-Carlton Club Level lounge working on this very chapter, at first it's what *doesn't* happen that is so impressive. The well-dressed, smiling club attendant *doesn't* come over to ask me if I want my coffee warmed up. Does this mean she's being inattentive? Quite the opposite. She sees that I am intently hammering out these very sentences and that it's a bad time to ask me anything. She remains ever observant, however, and is back and ready to serve as soon as I end the paragraph and lean back in my chair to ponder my next linguistic move.

This level of attentiveness, of empathetic and intuitive service, is phenomenal. But how do you transfer it to your own organization? To provide similarly skilled and nuanced service requires teaching your employees to pay attention to everything that is happening at the periphery of their senses and of their emotional awareness, what The Ritz-Carlton calls the principle of "Radar On—Antenna Up."

In addition, person-on-person service benefits from using a system, a framework that I've codified as the BUBL (pronounced "bubble") method. The awareness and behaviors represented in the BUBL acronym will assist you in interacting with guests in an effective and nuanced way.[1] The basis of BUBL, and the reason for the name, is the concept that each of your guests is surrounded by an individual, invisible, protective bubble. To be able to provide exceptional guest service, your team needs to be aware of this phenomenon and be conscious of the extent to which a guest's individual protective shell is open or closed at any particular moment. Employees need to learn to recognize when it's okay to venture near and into the guest's protective bubble—the invisible "meditation chapel" within which the guest has expectations of solitude—and how to interact with the guest while that bubble is open. This is what the well-trained attendant at The Ritz-Carlton club lounge is doing when she discreetly avoids interrupting me mid-thought, and it's also what she's doing when she reverses course and provides me with service as soon as it's clear to her that she won't be interrupting.

Here are the steps of the BUBL method:

B: Begin immediately
U: Un-code the guest's messages and pacing
B: Break your schedule
L: Leave room for more interaction

Let's take these one by one.

- ***Begin immediately:*** The guest expects service to begin *the exact moment* that she comes into contact with the employee, so deciphering whether or not the guest actually considers meaningful contact to have been made is an important part of this step. For example, if a guest catches a server's eye, it may be merely accidental, but if the guest *holds* the server's gaze, it usually means that the guest's expecting to be offered assistance. (At busy times, the "begin immediately" step may need to be accomplished even if the employee's busy speaking with another customer. This requires learning to work with one customer while visually acknowledging the presence of a new arrival.)

- *Un-code:* (The word, I know, should be "Decode," but that leaves us with an acronym of "BDBL," which, though fun to try to pronounce, isn't as memorable a mnemonic device as "BUBL.") Decipher the messages the customer is giving you about her desired pacing of service, as well as her level of happiness or distress and other emotions, and adjust appropriately. (Such cues aren't only detectable in person, by the way; they can be discerned on the phone, in online chat, via videoconferencing, etc.)

- *Break your schedule:* Your customer has let you into her bubble, her "meditation chapel," for the moment. Drop what you're doing and work on what she needs. True service can never be a slave to checking things off in a predetermined order. Attending properly to a customer means adhering to the *customer's* schedule, not your own. This means, for example, waiting for a natural break in conversation before asking how a meal is tasting, rather than barging in when your guest's in animated discourse or mid-bite into a juicy burger, just because she's next in the order you had in mind as you started your rounds, and you don't want to be delayed.

- *Leave room for more:* Is this really goodbye? Check before you conclude the interaction. It's the service professional's responsibility to ask if anything additional is needed and, if it isn't, to graciously thank the customer before leaving her to her solitary sanctuary.

At the Center of the Customer's Universe

The reason that such subtle aspects of service make a difference is because a guest wants to feel like they're at the center of your world. And, as a service provider, there's a lot of power in creating this impression. In a sense, this will have to be an illusion that you're creating, because in reality you have—I'm making some assumptions here—a life of your own and more than one guest to support. But it's an extremely powerful, business-building illusion for the hospitality professional who can successfully pull it off.

Guests are already at the center of their own world, their own reality. All that matters to them are themselves and the people they care about, a category that probably only tangentially includes you. What they want from you as a service provider is not for you to grab center stage, but to reassure them that they hold center stage in your world as well as in their own.

PUTTING THE CUSTOMER AT THE CENTER IN A LIMITED-SERVICE SETTING

"When I drill down to why we get the great TripAdvisor scores and comments that we do," says Rupesh Patel, the owner of two midscale and economy properties in Daytona Beach, Florida, "it's never about our lobbies or our furnishings—it's about our employees and how central they made the guests feel in the hospitality experience. Even within the limitations of our budgets and staffing, we do many little things to make the guest feel at the center of our operation at our hotels, small touches that are directly focused on the goal of making every guest feel special: custom candy bars and water bottles with the guest's name on it, for example, as well as welcome letters that are customized for each guest. We're not The Ritz-Carlton, but we can treat our guests as if we were, within the context of our limited service environment. And it works."

The Red Bench Principle

Years ago, my wife and I took our daughter to her first half day of nursery school. On that fine New England morning, the young teacher collected our daughter from us outside the classroom, where we were sitting together on a red park bench. When the teacher brought our daughter back to us at noon, my wife and I were again sitting on that same red bench. It wasn't until two or three weeks later, as the routine continued, that we figured out that our daughter believed her parents were sitting on that red bench each day throughout the entire morning, awaiting her return. She didn't think this in a vague or metaphorical sense. She didn't kind of partially believe this. She *really* believed it.

I find this a good reminder of the nature of the relationship of a business to its guests. Because guests, even adults, generally share these dependent-child qualities, the last thing they're considering are the other obligations, interests, or activities of their service providers. Guests assume, until you prove them wrong (which would be a mistake) that your world revolves around them—all the way and all the time. And as a hospitality provider, you benefit from encouraging this impression rather than becoming resentful that a guest is presumptuous enough to be thinking this way. It's a credit to your business, and to your level of service, if they believe that you're truly all about them all the time.

So I'm going to suggest you throw out the clichéd image of "rolling out the red carpet" and replace it with "sitting on the red bench" as the ultimate in customer care. In other words, what's most important isn't so much to put on an all-star show for your guests (though that can be great as well) as it is to create and maintain the illusion that you are always there awaiting your guest, attending to her as if you had nothing else on your agenda that could possibly interfere. Pull this off and you're well on your way to guaranteeing yourself a guest for life.

The Last Customer on Earth

Maintaining and advocating this "treat each customer like the last customer on earth" attitude is one of the most important leadership responsibilities in a hospitality organization, one of the key weapons in the battle to avoid losing guests through your perceived indifference, and one of the attitudes and advocacies that every single hospitality leader represented in this book shines in promoting.

Hospitality professional Bill Quiseng: "Whether it's acknowledging a guest as they're walking down the hall or using a guest's name at the hostess station, every interaction is a chance to make a guest feel cared for or to feel otherwise. And after every single interaction, the guest is making that determination of whether they were or weren't cared for." Restaurateur Danny Meyer, a legend of hospitality in New York (and now globally, thanks to the unparalleled success of his Shake Shack restaurant chain) shares the same sentiment, though he phrases it like a New Yorker: "Hospitality will not succeed unless the person on the receiving end knows all the way to the bottom of their *kishkes* [Yiddish for "guts"] that we're on their side. The definition of hospitality for me is the degree to which [the guest] feels that we are on their side, we have their back, we are their agent."

Meyer goes on to contrast this with the emotional disconnection customers often experience in the world of service:

> *Of course, [as consumers] we all have experiences that are the opposite of that, whether it's getting a cup of coffee or shopping at a department store: The service, technically speaking, is quite good; the provider does all the things they're supposed to do—yet it doesn't feel great. Or when I'm on an airplane, I arrive alive and on time. I get the drink I asked for. But the problem is that I don't get anything more. Not one person looks me in the eye while they're wheeling the cart down the aisle; nobody smiles or makes me feel that I'm anything more than somebody occupying a seat.*

Although these inattentive service interactions are, of course, not pleasant to experience as a customer, their frequency represents an upside for service professionals who are serious about one-guest-at-a-time service. The inattention of the rest of the business community represents an enormous competitive advantage; their affronts to the general customer population make the superior service of great hospitality organizations and professionals sparkle in contrast.

ERIC RIPERT: THE ESSENCE OF HOSPITALITY IS DIFFERENTIATION

"I didn't give a damn what the customer wanted when I was younger," confesses legendary chef Eric Ripert. "The only thing I cared about was my food—my vision as a chef. . . . I've since changed my ways," says Ripert, "because I realized that was the wrong way to go about things in a restaurant, and the wrong way to be as a person as well. It can never be just about the food."

Chef Ripert's commitment to food, of course, is unflagging. Le Bernardin, the New York institution where Ripert is Executive Chef, has retained a four star designation from *The New York Times* for an unparalleled thirty years and commands three stars from Michelin as well, in part because "We've upheld our particular reputation for food," as Ripert puts it modestly. Yet Le Bernardin, insists Ripert, is "in the hospitality business above all else."

Hospitality and Millennials

A temple of delicious hedonism like Le Bernardin is probably not what first comes to mind when you think of a millennial dining destination, but, says Ripert, "It's the millennials who have me excited now, who are stimulating my passion for hospitality. Being 100 percent committed to hospitality is important when you're thinking about millennials and the experience that they want and insist on." What millennials are looking for "is something that money almost cannot buy," something that is more than "a piece of fish," even an extraordinarily sourced and sauced fish. "It's not going to work with the millennial customer to be inhospitable. They're not going to take it if you come across as having an ego, an attitude, a lack of caring."

Differentiated Hospitality

For guests of any age, millennial or otherwise, says Ripert, true hospitality has to be *differentiated* hospitality. At Le Bernardin, "It's our responsibility to understand the need of the guest, to deliver an experience that's individually crafted for each individual in the dining room."

This means that Le Bernardin doesn't necessarily fawn all over what other businesses might consider to be their "VIP" customers; the Le Bernardin approach to service is more subtle than that. "Le Bernardin is thought of as a destination, a place people come to have an out of the ordinary experience, but that's too much of a generalization. We have regulars, people who come two, three times a week," from their nearby offices or because they come to the neighborhood to conduct business. It would be jarring to these regulars if Le Bernardin made a production out of their every visit, so the restaurant makes a point of treating them in a manner that's more as if they were members of a local club, whose repeated presence at the restaurant, while still appreciated, is an expected occurrence. "The local businessman doesn't care about visiting the kitchen and taking pictures with the chef," says Ripert, and the restaurant is scrupulous about not suggesting such activities to them. There's also a contingent of guests whom Le Bernardin attracts who are wealthy (often international) travelers "who like to eat in this kind of restaurant but don't like much interaction with the staff; we have to be careful to step back from them for this reason."

Still, "The majority of our customers are the ones who come to have a celebration or an experience." But even within this experience-seeking clientele," there are key distinctions to be made. "There are couples who come in for an experience, but who are so in love that they end up not seeing anything but each other. They don't want to be interrupted more than necessary, and they certainly don't want to come into the kitchen and take pictures." What they want, instead, "is a space for themselves, a bubble. Though they appreciate what we do in the restaurant, it's all about being together, the two of them."

Another contingent of bubble-enclosed customers are "the guests where the event they're celebrating, the birthday or the closing of a deal, is really the focus, not us." There are also, of course, many guests at the opposite spectrum, "customers who thrive on taking pictures with the chef, and on a lot of interaction with us." And then there are the foodies: "Le Bernardin is a place of celebration for foodies as well." Like others, the "foodies may want pictures with the chef and all of that, but they are most about the fish and the different flavors and the details of the menu."

If the restaurant gets all this right, concludes Ripert, "If we make them happy in the particular way they were looking to be made happy, they'll remember Le Bernadin and want to come back at their next opportunity. But to pull this off, we almost have to read the minds of the guest, to make sure we don't mistakenly end up providing the wrong kind of experience for them."

The How's and the Who's of Reading Minds

To allow the restaurant to read a room in such a subtle a manner and with so much at stake, Le Bernadin relies on dining room employees who have a long tenure (Ben Chekroun, Le Bernardin's dining room manager, has been in his position more than twenty years) and who are innately suited to the task of mindreading. Ripert says that "Many times the people I get for these positions have been recommended to me by other restaurants who notice this ability in them that we value here, people who will thrive working in our dining room."

Having said that, Ripert feels that mindreading "doesn't take a genius—it mostly takes *wanting* to do it. Even I," he continues with characteristic modesty, "although I'm a cook, I'm not front of the house, when I cross the dining room I can tell when I look at a table who's a foodie, who's not a foodie, who's here for a business function, who cares about seeing the chef. You can see it in their behavior and in their eyes—the eyes that follow you wherever you go. You don't have to be a genius to see that. You just have to actually look, and you have to be focused on our shared goal at Le Bernardin, which, above all, is this: We want to provide *not* the experience we think the customer should have, but the experience the customer—the single customer in front of us—wants to have this evening."

I can't wrap a bow around this chapter and allow us to move on without conceding something important: You *can't* always perform at a "last customer on Earth" level—although it's a level you can always aspire to. It is absolutely true that delivering this superior service to one guest at a time, without inconveniencing the rest of your guests who also want your assistance and attention, can be a significant challenge, involving investments in training, processes, and technology. In fact, you will not be able to execute a "last customer on Earth" approach to your satisfaction all the time. But if you don't actively, emphatically follow and believe in this approach, you'll end up compromising on the service you provide and not even realizing that you're doing this.

If you set out explicitly to do business the "last customer on Earth" way, while you may at times be forced to compromise your service ideal—because of limitations of time, staffing, technology, or other resources—when this happens, you'll feel the entire weight of the discrepancy. You'll know you're not living up to your ideal, and you will be motivated to work on the staffing, systems, technology, and processes that can bring you closer to the ideal.

"AND YOUR POINT IS"?

Key Principles from Chapter 1:
The Last Customer on Earth

▶ Great hospitality must be focused on one guest at a time. For the moments that you are together, treat every guest as if she were the only customer in the world.

▶ For all of the best intentions that most of us start out with in our businesses, it's nearly inevitable that a high level of caring about the customer slips when customer numbers increase. And this loss directly sabotages the future growth of your company. The way to prevent too much slippage in standards is to be determined that you and your organization maintain the mindset that *"If we did it right for our first guest, we'll find a way to keep doing it for our millionth,* one on one, without rushing or cutting corners."

▶ The BUBL method of serving customers: An important concept is that every guest is surrounded by an individual, invisible protective bubble. Your team needs to learn to recognize when it's okay to venture into the customer's protective bubble—and how to interact with the customer while that bubble is open. The BUBL method suggests the following:

Begin immediately to have the interaction when the occasion arises.

Un-code (decode) the guest's messages and pacing.

Break your schedule—be flexible and take advantage of opportunities for interaction.

Leave room for additional interaction before ending the service interaction.

2

Systems and Standards: The Secret Weapons of Service

"Behind-the-scenes work is just as important as a polite host
or knowledgeable server."

—STEPHEN STARR, owner, STARR Restaurants

To the eyes of your guest, a great hospitality experience should look like it was a cinch to pull off. To the extent that your efforts are even noticed, great hospitality should appear to be the result of a group of thoughtful employees spontaneously choosing to do their jobs quickly, efficiently, and cheerfully.

However, to deliver service with any level of consistency, your organization is going to require a set of standards, behaviors, preparations, and execution points—and these aren't going to happen by accident or without effort. To be great at hospitality means to excel at building and maintaining standards and systems that allow your business to create a repeatable result for its customers across a wide variety of situations and with a changing cast of employees.

Part I: Standards

Let's look at standards first. A standard is anything from a tactic to help you do your job more easily (how to efficiently slice a lime) to a brand consistency standard (how quickly to answer the telephone and the specific greeting to use when you do so). Today, The Ritz-Carlton Hotel Company has approximately 3,000 brand standards that it strives to maintain across its 90 hotels worldwide, says Diana Oreck, who helms The Ritz-Carlton Leadership Center, the division tasked with sharing Ritz-Carlton methodology with companies in other industries. (They're the organization, in fact, that Steve Jobs turned to when opening the Apple Stores.)

Oreck elaborates:

> *Of these 3,000 brand standards, there are a different number of standards that apply per department. As an employee, you're responsible for knowing every standard that applies to your department. For example, if you work at the front desk, you'll know that our standard for answering the phone is "within three rings." If you're a bartender, you'll know our particular standards for how to garnish each type of cocktail.*
>
> *Some standards are simply strategies that allow you to do your job in the best way possible [for example, how to set and clear a table]; others are brand consistency standards; for example, in our bathrooms we use Asprey soaps. These are the details that make up our brand voice. Maybe they sound unimportant, but if you walked into the bath in your guestroom and you found that the local Ritz-Carlton had provided Neutrogena, it would feel like we had lost a bit of our brand voice.*

In case this level of devotion to standards strikes you as pointlessly over the top, consider the following. As I was finishing up this manuscript, the JD Power organization announced[2] that The Ritz-Carlton had achieved this year's highest customer satisfaction ranking in luxury travel and had beaten its *own* most recent and top-in-the-field ranking for customer satisfaction by a significant margin. Although it's hard to prove a causal relationship—not to mention the validity of any particular ranking system—this strikes me as a pretty encouraging indicator that the work spent obsessing over these three thousand "picky" standards has been valid and valuable.

The Click of a Door, and the Story That It Tells

Across town in the lair of Ritz-Carlton's arch-nemesis, Four Seasons Hotels and Resorts, you can sense *this* company's obsession with standards just by taking the time to listen to the click of your guest room door as it closes. That click, the reassuringly solid sound that you take for granted as a guest when you absentmindedly close your hotel room door, is an example of why Four Seasons is Four Seasons, and most organizations aren't even close.

Let me start this story at the beginning.[3] A friend of mine was halfway down the hallway heading toward the elevator at a Four Seasons hotel when he realized he'd forgotten his briefcase. Walking back toward his room, he saw to his surprise that a maintenance engineer had propped the door open and was adjusting its closing mechanism.

Being a curious lad, my friend decided to find out what was going on. The engineer told him, "The housekeeper servicing the room next door noticed that when your door closes, it closes with an indeterminate, gentle closing sound, less definitive than the 'click' we prefer, so she called down to engineering to have us come up and adjust the closing mechanism."

As I see it, there are three standards that Four Seasons is displaying and enforcing here:

- *Standard 1: A guest room door should make a specific sound when it closes.* Four Seasons doesn't like a guest room door to close with a bang, and it doesn't like it to close with a whimper; it should have a definitive yet understated "click." That such a standard even exists is a good reminder that a properly constructed hospitality experience is the product of all the customer's senses and emotions: what the guest hears, feels, tastes, even (for better or worse) smells, and that company standards should cover the spectrum of these senses. In the case of its

door-click standard, Four Seasons is attempting to maintain a sound that creates an emotion of wellbeing; the
solid, unequivocal click represents security to the guest,
the ability to know, without even looking back, that the
door has closed securely.

- *Standard 2: Defects should be reported, even across
organizational and functional lines.* Everything the
housekeeper did to set this story in motion is something
that in almost any other organization would be deemed
"not her job." Yet she, in fact, thinks it *is* her job and uses
her awareness, time, and effort to first note and then act
on the details of the click of a door on a room she wasn't
even assigned to clean. (Remember, this was the room
next door to the room she was cleaning.)

    Let's pause for a moment here, to allow me some time
atop my soapbox. Energizing and empowering employees
to engage in purpose-driven, cross-functional behavior is
an incredibly important part of great hospitality. If you
focus your employees only on their directly assigned functions—cleaning a particular room, for example—you're
not only doing a disservice to your guests, but you're wasting your employees' human potential. Housekeepers can
be so much more than rote vacuumers. They can also be a
force for safety, security, and much more. And this is true
of every employee in your organization; when they are
encouraged to use more of their brain and heart cells they
will be happier and stay longer.

- *Standard 3: Conform to the guest's schedule, no matter how much that inconveniences you.* The Four Seasons doesn't schedule guest room repairs at the hotel's

convenience. In fact, it schedules them in the absolutely least convenient way for the hotel: conforming them to the guest's schedule. The front desk didn't call my friend and say, "When do you think you'll be leaving your room so we can perform some maintenance?" (Believe me, many hotels do.) The staff didn't wait until the room was turning over. They hurried to make the repair during the course of his stay (so he would have the benefit of the clicking door), yet scheduled it for a time that should have made their repair efforts entirely invisible to him. (Of course, they also made sure that his "Please make up the room" light was lit before entering.) This required an elaborate choreography of the housekeeper noticing he was gone and slipping engineering into the mix at exactly the right moment.

Part II: Systems

Let's move on from service standards to the more elaborate concept of service systems. By "systems" I don't mean "technology," although technology can be an important part of a well-designed service system. By "service system," I mean any action or set of actions that a business executes consistently to make the experience of doing business with it better: e.g., warmer, faster, safer, easier, or more engaging. This definition comes to us courtesy of Jay Coldren, VP of EDITION Hotels, the innovative luxury collaboration between Marriott and noted/notorious hotelier Ian Schrager. I like Jay's definition a lot, but alternatively, you may want to forget all about formal definitions and just imagine the following sticky scenario as an easy way to grasp what service systems look like.

It's hot outside, you're at a theme park, and you're craving ice cream. You wait in line for fifteen minutes that feel like forty, wrangle with family members, choose your flavors, fork over your payment, and step away, triumphant, from the ice cream counter. Then it happens: You drop your cone—you do a total cone-plant on the amusement park midway. It's such a simple, prosaic accident, but it can blemish your whole day and the memories you take home with you of your park experience. Which is why, when I dropped an ice-cream cone smack in the middle of the midway of a Six Flags theme park, a look at what happened next provides such a good lesson in the systematic side of providing hospitality.

The Six Flags crew sprang into action, replacing it for me immediately, without my needing to ask, without another wait in line, and at no charge. They salvaged the day for me, as well as for my family with whom I was visiting the park and who were briefly threatened with a very mopey Micah.[4]

Six Flags prepares its employees systematically to watch for predictable stress points in a guest's day and it has systems at the ready to turn those experiences into something positive. So in their response to the ice cream-spillage incident, they weren't just being merciful on an ad hoc basis. This was *procedural* for them; it was a preplanned service recovery involving janitorial services workers to take care of the spill and coworkers to step in and cover the register while the young lady was remaking my cone, and so forth. Their reaction to such stress points (and many others) is informed by how Six Flags sees itself. "We're not just in the business of having the tallest, fastest, most thrilling rides," CEO Jim Reid-Anderson tells me. "We're in the business of making people happy." And as with ride engineering and maintenance, guest happiness depends on having the systems to support it.

Customer service systems can be divided broadly into five categories:

1. **Preparation:** Processes that help clear the way for a great service experience, prior to its delivery.

2. **Execution:** Systems that help employees during their customer interactions and that enable them to consistently provide a high level of service.

3. **Guest preference and experience tracking:** Systems that enhance the guest experience by making it more personally

appropriate. (While, alternatively, I could place these systems into either the "preparation" or "execution" category, I find it helpful to consider them separately.)

4. **Recovery:** Systems for handling those times when things go wrong.

5. **Continuous improvement:** Systems for making the next service encounter even better than this one.

Category 1: Preparation

Preparatory customer service systems involve a variety of behind-the-scenes disciplines: engineering, finance and accounting, shipping and receiving, purchasing, training, continuous education, and, of course, HR. As far as guest-facing employees, some of the preparatory steps that are the most important are product knowledge (for example, familiarity with the major ingredients in popular menu items and with fire evacuation procedures); technical know-how, such as mastering knife skills and knowing the back-preserving ways to lift luggage; and the understanding of psychological skills required to get employees into the right mindset for when it's "go time" and the guests arrive. Role-playing exercises (for example, simulating an interaction with a guest with disabilities who needs special services on a busy cruise check-in day) fall in this category as well, as does one of the most important preparatory systems of all, the daily pre-shift lineup, discussed in Chapter 4, "Building a Culture of Yes."

Category 2: Execution

Your company's ability to perform in front of your guests is where the rubber meets the roadmap in the world of hospitality. Customer service systems that kick in during the real-time execution of the hospitality experience are integral to delivering superior hospitality. These systems can sometimes be quite technical; Caesars Entertainment manages to find a way to sew radio frequency identification (RFID) tags into its cocktail servers' uniforms—don't ask me where!—which are then scanned as the servers enter and exit the bar, in the interest of improving staffing and flow decisions. Often, though, it's simpler, nontechnical systems that save the day by helping employees do their best work. Systems such as the "4 S" framework—*stop, stand, smile, and offer a salutation*—help the employees of Montage Resorts provide consistently good service whenever they encounter a guest. Craig Schoninger, Director of Sales and Marketing at Palmetto Bluff, one of the notable properties in the Montage portfolio, explains: "4S keeps us from getting sloppy or from appearing to get sloppy. Great service is easy to provide now and again, but to provide it every time, we depend on systematic frameworks such as our '4 S.'"

Category 3: Guest Preference and Experience Tracking

One of the keys to flawless execution is an accurate and updatable guest preference tracking system. Such systems don't have to be complicated. When Ritz-Carlton started building such a system, it did so with notepads and a goal of noting just five preferences per guest and satisfying three or more of these preferences on every subsequent visit at whatever Ritz-Carlton in the world that guest might travel to next. This allowed Ritz-Carlton to create a hotel company at which, wherever in the world you stayed, you were ensured of a stay that was customized in ways that related to you as a person and to what you had enjoyed on previous stays.[5] Of course, Ritz-Carlton has expanded its system since the days of notepad scribbling, but it still follows the same principles. Diana Oreck, Vice President of The Ritz-Carlton Leadership Center, explains how the Mystique system, as it's now called, works:

> *Whenever we discover or are alerted to a guest's preferences, we put them into Mystique, and Mystique talks to all the properties within Ritz-Carlton. As a guest, you can go from Ritz-Carlton to*

Ritz-Carlton around the world, and we will know and be able to deliver what you like.

A lot of these guest preferences come from observation and listening. It wouldn't be as magical if we just gave you a legal pad and said, "Hey, what do you like?" We'd rather use Mystique to increase a guest's sense of wonder, with little things delivered unexpectedly: If we saw that every day you seemed to be eating chocolate, or we saw that you'd bought two six packs of Diet Coke, the housekeeper would enter that.

A similar approach works in food service. One such preference-tracking systems in the F&B world is employed at John Meadow's LDV Hospitality, a sprawling organization of more than twenty restaurants with brands that include Scarpetta, American Cut, and Dolce Italian. In each of LDV's locations, frequent guests are coded and their dining preferences are kept on file. This is accomplished with the assistance of servers, managers, and hosts who make note of preferences that they observe in their patrons (perhaps a wine, cocktail, or meat temperature preference) and enter them in the diners' profiles. These are compiled into an internal database and linked across all LDV properties, regardless of brand. "For example," Meadow tells me, "if you're a regular at Scarpetta and you favor a particular martini, that will be flagged in the system so when you visit The Regent Cocktail Club in Miami, the drink will be ready for you upon arrival." Similar to The Ritz-Carlton's goal with its Mystique system, Meadow is a believer in "using extra touches of surprise service" to enhance his guests' experience. However, LDV Hospitality employees such as the warm and personable Noé Alarcon, Wine Director at Scarpetta in Las Vegas, are scrupulous about keeping such technological enhancements out of view of the customer, integrating them with the human-delivered service as invisibly as possible. The result is intended to be a net gain thanks to deploying both humanity and technology, rather than the incomplete replacement that technology alone would provide.

Tracking the experience of your guests *while* they are experiencing your hospitality is a master touch you should consider adding to your repertoire as well. When you have a system that alerts you to glitches that come up in the course of a guest's visit, it allows you to follow up later in the visit to ensure that all was handled well and that your guest feels well cared for. For instance, in the (rare) event a guest at Four Seasons encounters a problem early in their stay, not only is the glitch addressed immediately, but later in their stay the guest will be greeted by a manager as follows: "I understand there was a challenge early in your stay. I wanted to follow up and see how things are going and whether I can be of further assistance," which is much more sensitive than a know-nothing follow-up like, "How's everything going, great?"

This kind of thinking doesn't always have to involve post-glitch recovery, and it doesn't only apply to lodging. Patrick O'Connell's dining room staff at The Inn at Little Washington has taken this real-time approach in a unique direction with a "mood-tracking" system so unusual that it has been covered by the *Harvard Business Review*. O'Connell's dining room employees discreetly (*very* discreetly) make note of the apparent happiness level of every guest at a table as they are sitting down and throughout the course of their dining experience. The goal, by the end of the evening, is to massage the elements of the dining experience in ways that will raise the happiness level of every single guest to at least a "nine" on a scale of one to ten. If a guest isn't clicking with a particular waiter, if they need additional attention, if they seem to be regretfully eyeing the entrée they passed up when ordering—whatever, in the judgment of the waitstaff, could be changed to improve the situation—they go ahead and make that change. They switch out the waiter, send Chef O'Connell or one of his managers over to lavish additional attention, bring over an appetizer-sized portion of the Entrée Not Ordered . . .

(For a look at an entirely different, electronic way to keep tabs on guest satisfaction in real time, even when the guest is barricaded alone in their

hotel room, see my discussion in chapter 9 of Ivy, an opt-in text-based system powered by Watson, IBM's legendary artificial intelligence brain.)

Category 4: Service Recovery

No matter how hard you try, eventually your organization, or your guests, or some uncontrollable force like the weather is bound to throw a monkey wrench (or perhaps a monkey—in hospitality, you're going to see it all) into the works. A great service organization will recognize these inevitabilities and establish systems for handling a wide variety of service calamities, systems that allow your employees to represent your organization in the best possible light during these moments of stress.

If you're in the restaurant business, for example, you know that it's only a matter of time before someone spills something on one of your guests. You also know that sooner or later a waiter is going to ring in the wrong order, a chef will cook steak to the wrong temperature, a bottle of wine will be corked. Great restaurants distinguish themselves by having clearly defined fixes for common problems: solutions on which the entire staff is trained. Having these fixes in place allows the staff to handle common problems with ease and grace. And when these fixes go above and beyond the guests' expectations, it can turn these glitches into opportunities to generate amazing word of mouth.

Consider another example from the dining room of The Inn at Little Washington. When a guest spills a glass of red wine in the dining room of The Inn (making a mess of the beautiful linen tabletop and causing distress for the diners), something remarkable happens. The *entire* service staff stops whatever they are doing, practically in mid-motion, and hurries over to help completely refresh and reset the table. Two staff members clear the table, while another fetches and spreads a new tablecloth. Two others place an entirely new set of dishes and glassware, while the sommelier replaces the glass of wine. The food is refreshed or replated in the kitchen and, at the very end, the flowers are placed back on the table. The

Inn calls this an "Emergency Clear" and uses it to transform what could be a protracted and embarrassing moment of mess and confusion into a two-minute flurry of choreographed activity that leaves guests open-mouthed in awe.

A Framework for Service Recovery

Tablecloth heroics aside, most service recoveries can benefit from following a specific response framework. In fact, I'm going to brazenly offer up my very own five-step service recovery framework for your consideration: **A**pologize, **R**eview, **F**ix and **F**ollow Up, and **D**ocument (Sorry folks: all that spells is 'ARFFD.' If you prefer, you can use Marriott's LEARN: Listen, Empathize, Apologize, Respond, and Notify. Or The Broadmoor's HEART: Hear, Empathize, Apologize, Respond, Take Action, and Follow up. But I like my humble ARFFD just fine.

Here are the steps to take when responding to a service failure:[6]

- *Apologize* **and ask for forgiveness.** And make it a real apology, not a fake "I'm sorry if you feel that way." What's needed here is a sincere, personal, non-mechanical apology. Convey that you recognize and regret what your customer has been through. The key to an effective apology, to getting back on the right foot with your customer, is to convey from the very outset that you are going to take the guest's side and share the guest's viewpoint. (Please note that you may be apologizing for a situation, rather than for something that is your fault. Regardless, express your sorrow, your regrets, for the situation that is affecting the customer's experience.)

- *Review* **the complaint with your guest.** Give your guest a chance to explain what's gone wrong from the *guest's* view and what they think you should do to fix it.

- **Fix the problem and then *follow up*.** Either fix the issue in the next twenty minutes (in a lodging situation; in an F&B situation you have to move much faster) or follow up within twenty minutes to check on the guest and explain the progress you have made. Follow up *after* fixing things as well, to show continuing concern and appreciation.

- **Document the problem in detail.** This allows you to permanently fix the defect by identifying the underlying issues involved.

Before we're done with ARFFD, let's take one more look at the first step, the apology. I want to share a technique, the "Italian Mama," that goes back to my first book, *Exceptional Service, Exceptional Profit*, my collaboration with service and hospitality expert Leonardo Inghilleri, who is Italian down to his toes. Together we suggest the archetype of an adoring Italian mother and the way she'd react if her toddler took a tumble:

> *"Oh, my darling, look at what happened! Oh, you skinned your knee on that walkway, my bambino; let me kiss that terrible wound. Shall we watch a little TV? And here's a lollipop for you while I bandage you up!"*[7]

If you've spent much time around kids, or around guests, you'll know that this sort of response is quite disarming. The kid will push back with a "Ma, I'm not hurt that bad; can I just go back out and play now?" And as soon as a guest feels truly heard and feels your entire lack of defensiveness, the guest will likely move pretty quickly to a "Well, it's not really your fault and it's not the end of the world."

Now, let me caution you emphatically here: Not only is this a cartoonishly over-the-top illustration, but every guest is different and needs to be handled based on that guest's mood and demeanor. The point I am making is to *start* your response by addressing the *emotional* component of a service lapse and not giving your guest even a whiff of a "Let's sort out the facts and assign responsibility" attitude of a courtroom practitioner.

> *"Let's sort out the facts of the situation. What was the angle of the concrete in the sidewalk at time of impact, and were you wearing proper protective clothing per the user's manual at the time your knee impacted the concrete? And I need to ask, young man: were you exceeding the sidewalk speed limit?"* [8]

(For a less over-the-top pair of examples, compare the simple and lovely "I am really sorry to hear that happened!" with the instantly alienating, "And how's that our fault?")

Of course, there *is* a time for problem solving, which is what most of the steps in "ARFFD" relate to. But you don't want to rush into problem solving without addressing, at least for a moment, the emotional state of your upset customer.

Failures Result from Broken Systems

When the customer experience at your business goes bad, it's often because one or more of your customer service systems are broken or haven't been set up in the first place. A guest complains—in person if you're lucky, on TripAdvisor if you're not—about a lousy early-morning interaction with the front desk agent. Your first impulse is to bite the desk agent's head off, but I hope you'll hold that impulse, and your teeth, in check and look at the situation dispassionately. If you have the chance to study the performance of your desk agent, you'll likely discover a set of problems that goes something like this: your desk agent wasn't logged in to her terminal at the beginning of her shift, so she wasn't prepared to serve the first guest who walked up to her; she couldn't find a pen for the guest to sign the credit card slip; she seems to be generally disorganized.

WHEN SERVICE RECOVERY MEANS THE DIFFERENCE BETWEEN LIFE AND DEATH

Some hospitality mishaps go far beyond corked wine or an overcooked steak. I've heard more than one restaurant professional's sad story of a guest who literally died mid-service, and hoteliers, because of the realities of being open 24/7, have quite a few shocking experiences.

Tom Colicchio, the renowned restaurateur (Craft, Colicchio Brothers, etc.) and Top Chef judge, has over time developed a recovery system that has so far served him well for such life-and-death emergencies: Get yourself trained ahead of time, identify the nature of the situation (some emergencies may not be obvious), stay calm, and bring in professional assistance as soon as possible.

"Over the years," says Colicchio, "there have been a variety of emergencies in my restaurants—people having heart attacks, one guest with a bleeding ulcer who passed out on the floor, and so forth." In each case, he says, what's needed is pretty much the same: "You have to recognize the situation [as being an emergency], keep your head about you, defuse the situation—keep people in their seats rather than gathering around, call the paramedics right away, and use your first aid skills as needed."

All of this came into play in the most famous life-and-death moment of recent hospitality industry lore: the night Colicchio saved Joan Nathan, the cookbook author and television food personality, from choking at a food industry benefit gala.

I was in the doorway of the kitchen having a conversation with someone. I turned to my right and saw Joan apparently choking. I came up behind her, put my arms around her, and asked, "Can you talk?" She indicated "No." I did it [the Heimlich maneuver] once, which is not that difficult of a procedure; I learned it as a teenage lifeguard. "Can you talk now?" I asked again. Still, no. Second try, it came out. That was it. I asked if she was okay, she answered yes, and I went back to my conversation.

In other words, what you have is a failure of systems, including some or all of the following:

- *Training and preparation:* Why wasn't she prepped on the necessary supplies and log-in procedure for starting a shift? And going deeper than this, has she been instructed in one of the workplace organization systems, perhaps the workspace organization aspect of Lean Manufacturing methodology? (Lean, formerly known as the Toyota Production System, is an organizational philosophy and methodology that is well worth studying, although beyond the scope of this book. In fact, The Ritz-Carlton's defect-tracking system, Mr. Biv, which I'll discuss, is a simplified version of one aspect of Lean.)

- *Scheduling:* As a cost-control measure, was she told to show up at work the very minute her shift begins rather than a more realistic 15 to 30 minutes earlier, which would have allowed her to mentally settle in, get her bank ready to make change, organize her workspace, and so forth?

- *Employee selection:* Saying "there was a failure in hiring" is different from saying it's the employee's fault. If she is wrong for this position (not detail-oriented enough, for example) it's not *her* fault; it's the fault of the system that was responsible for selecting her.

A rule of thumb is that when something goes wrong once, it might be a specific employee's fault, or it could be just a fluke. If it happens twice, though, you should assume it's the fault of the system. Therefore, when you find repeated, identical mistakes, the solution is to revisit the system to see how it is designed and how it is, or isn't, being implemented.

In our example of the front desk agent, it's clear that a system needs to be developed to ensure that all supplies are stocked before each shift. This system could be in the form of a small checklist or a job description that defines the employee's role. Whatever way the organization chooses to deal with the situation is fine, as long as it solves the problem for good. The absolutely wrong approach is to yell at the front desk agent for being unprepared. Not only is this demoralizing for a good employee who is trying her best, but it also doesn't solve the problem systematically and in a sustainable manner.

How do you discover the systems in your company that are missing or poorly designed? There are systems for that as well (we'll get to that in a moment), but fundamentally it depends on building a culture where mistakes are embraced as learning opportunities and guest complaints as opportunities for improvement. Turning every issue that comes up into a witch hunt will drive your employees to focus more on covering up their mistakes than on solving problems and providing service. You need your employees to be comfortable telling you when they've slipped up so that such slips can be fixed in the future—systematically.

For example, Mayo Clinic, the great medical institution, wants incoming physicians to understand that they won't ever be blamed for admitting mistakes or for asking for help. But doing the opposite, taking the lone wolf approach of never asking for help or admitting a problem that might affect a patient, is potentially career-ending.[9]

Category 5: Continuous Improvement

Perhaps the most important system any organization can put in place is the one that allows the organization to identify flaws and improve itself over time. This type of system is both rare and important. In such a setup, employees are empowered—required, actually—to identify flaws in the guest experience, logging those flaws as they are discovered.

Let's take a look at "Mr. Biv," The Ritz-Carlton's easy-to-use tracking system. "Mr. Biv" stands for the five types of defects Ritz-Carlton wants to track:

+ *M*istakes
+ *R*eworks
+ *B*reakdowns
+ *I*nefficiencies
+ *V*ariations in work processes

Ritz-Carlton GM Liam Doyle (The Ritz-Carlton, Dove Mountain) explains how it works:

> *It's the responsibility of every employee and every manager to record any defect. Take, for example, a server reaching across the guest to pour wine: Our goal is that this will never get to the point of a guest noticing it; a manager on the floor or another waitstaff employee will be the one to notice and document the defect. Mr. Bivs are used only in a positive way; if we used them in a negative way, employees would never report them.*
>
> *Now, let me add some texture to my explanation. We consider some issues systemic, and some are just simple mistakes. If one steak is overcooked, that's a mistake, and we'd just alert the cook. If ten steaks are overcooked, that's a training issue, and in this case, we wouldn't take it to the cook but to the section leader to figure out what needs to be done to improve our cooks' training. Mr. Biv becomes healthy when everybody does it. You get stronger by dealing with your defects.*

Bill Quiseng, a hospitality and customer experience expert, has helmed a variety of marquee hotels. His beliefs on this subject will serve well to close out this chapter:

I am convinced you cannot begin to satisfy a single guest until you remove all the potential dissatisfiers. Each likely guest touchpoint should be examined to ensure that everything about it is optimal, thereby greatly reducing or even eliminating the likelihood of any negative incident. There's no other way to deliver on the promise of hospitality. And delivering on your promise is the only way to have your guests come to trust you.

"AND YOUR POINT IS"?

Key Principles from Chapter 2:
Systems and Standards: The Secret Weapons of Service

▶ While hospitality should appear effortless and spontaneous to the guest, behind that appearance you need service standards and service systems.

▶ Customer service standards range from tactics to help you do your job easier (how to efficiently slice a lime) to brand-consistency standards (how quickly to answer the telephone and what greeting to use).

▶ Customer service *systems* are more involved. They can be defined as "any action or set of actions that a business executes consistently to make the experience of doing business with it better: e.g., warmer, faster, safer, easier, or more engaging."

▶ Customer service systems can be divided roughly into five categories:
  + preparation
  + execution
  + guest preference and experience tracking
  + recovery
  + continuous improvement

▶ Preparatory systems improve the real-time execution of the hospitality experience once it's "go time" and you're on stage with the guest.

▶ Mishaps are inevitable in any service situation, and many of these mishaps fit predictable patterns (a guest will spill wine on the tablecloth). Great hospitality organizations distinguish themselves by having clearly defined fixes that the entire staff is trained to do.

▶ Most service recoveries can benefit from following a specific response framework.

    ✦ **Apologize** and ask for forgiveness.

    ✦ **Review** the complaint with your customer.

    ✦ **Fix** the problem and **follow up**, both internally to ensure the fix happened, and with the customer to ensure they're pleased with the resolution.

    ✦ **Document** the problem in detail.

▶ When you have a customer experience failure at your business, strive to fix the system, rather than blaming the employee.

▶ Build a culture where mistakes are embraced as learning opportunities and guest complaints as opportunities for improvement. If employees are blamed for errors they will cover up their mistakes rather than identifying them and improving them.

▶ The most important system an organization can deploy is one that allows the organization to identify flaws and improve itself over time.

3

People Are the Heart of Hospitality

"In the bad old 'personnel department' days, you'd hear that adage of 'Don't get too close to your employees.' Well, we live by an almost opposite philosophy at The Broadmoor. We **want** our managers to be as close as possible to their employees, not in terms of fraternization, but in terms of getting to know them, helping with their career aspirations, and providing them guidance and opportunities to help them better themselves."

—STEVE BARTOLIN, Chairman of The Broadmoor

n some industries, "People are our most important resource" is the most cynical of platitudes, ignored as openly as, say, "Safety is our first priority." But in the hospitality industry, no truer words could ever be spoken. A hospitality organization can't succeed until it learns to effectively recruit, retain, and develop employees.

Some hospitality leaders even object to using common terms that they feel reduce the importance of employees. There is nearly universal objection, for example, to the simple word "hiring" and a preference to replace it with the term and concept of "selecting." Herve Humler, President and COO of The Ritz-Carlton Hotel Company, explains: "You don't just 'hire' people, you carefully *select* them."

Brad Black, President and CEO of HUMANeX a company renowned for hiring (oops, *selecting)* employees for organizations in hospitality and other service-intensive industries, says, "We select; we don't just "hire." The distinction is important. It's like selecting members of an Olympic team, as opposed to hiring from whoever is standing on a job lot."

But nomenclature is the least of the improvements to be made here. To become one of the greats of hospitality, strive, in employee recruiting, selection, onboarding and development, to follow what I consider to be six guiding principles:

1. Select employees systematically.
2. Select them from the largest possible applicant pool
3. Tell employees what you want from them—because otherwise, you'll never get it.
4. Thoughtless onboarding sinks ships.
5. Take an integrated approach to employee development.
6. Employees should be involved in designing how their work is carried out.

Principle 1: Employee Selection Must Be Systematic

In a people-oriented business, you need to have the right people. So who are these "right people"? While different positions may require different technical aptitudes and skills, the universal requirement for employees in a hospitality organization is that they have the right *traits* for service. Barring this, you're spit out of luck.

Here's why trait-based hiring is so crucial:

Personality traits are, to a significant extent, fixed in place by the time applicants reach their twenties. In other words, it's hard to *make* people like other people, to make them empathic, or to convince people to enjoy being part of a team. Restaurateur Danny Meyer explains it this way: "If you have the right hospitality quotient [the six personality traits he lays out later in this chapter] but lack technical knowledge, that doesn't worry us. We think we can do a pretty effective job at helping you to improve technically. We're concerned, on the other hand, about hiring anyone without those emotional skills, because those are pretty much baked into people by the time we meet them and are a lot less teachable."

Ann Alba, resident manager at The Broadmoor, the longest running five star resort in the world (now boasting a *triple* five star rating, i.e., five stars for accommodations, five for the dining at their Penrose Room, and five for their spa) is similarly concerned with finding people who can be nice and who also enjoy being nice. "To be nice to people and be 'onstage' 24/7, you have to love what you're doing. Eventually it becomes evident which employees are trying to fake this passion, and we'd rather never get to that point of on-the-job discovery. So we try to find out the emotional truth earlier, via our hiring process."

You can't send people to "smile classes." As Patrick O'Connell says, the first test for a position at his Inn at Little Washington is this: "Does the applicant smile easily?" If he doesn't, he's "unlikely to instinctively know how to put others at ease, which is an invaluable trait in service" that's hard to compensate for, no matter how much training is piled on in the attempt.

Restaurateur Tom Colicchio thinks of this as a sort of dinner party divide: "We're looking to find people who *naturally* enjoy this work. The best way I can describe the people we want is like this: There are some people who throw great dinner parties because they really want to take care of their guests, and there are other people who are lousy at it because everything is a chore—everything is a problem. We're looking for that natural host, the person who is always looking to make people happy and who doesn't find it to be a chore."

- **You can't count on hiring people who have already been trained elsewhere.** In fact, this can be counterproductive. O'Connell again weighs in: "Bad habits are not given up easily. If a great deal of 'unlearning' has to take place, we find it more arduous than dealing with a clean slate." Or, as hospitality and customer experience expert Bill Quiseng puts it, "Hire the heart. Train the brain."

Bring Science into the Selection

Now, let's talk about how to find the people who possess the right traits for hospitality, and let's get specific about what those hospitable traits actually are.

The Broadmoor is a century-old destination hotel and resort that dominates the landscape in Colorado Springs, Colorado. It employs an astonishing 2,300 employees at high season (1,800 year-round) to service its nearly 900 hotel rooms and nine on-site restaurants and to staff its famous spa. Employee selection, as you can imagine, is central to the success of the entire Broadmoor operation, and for this purpose, The Broadmoor employs a scientific assessment/profiling tool developed by Predictive Index. "What we're looking for with our Predictive Index assessment tool," says Steve Bartolin, The Broadmoor's chairman, "are people who are hospitable by nature, who are positive, energetic, and kind. You give us that, and we can work with you."

At the 90 hotels and resorts managed worldwide by Ritz-Carlton, they make use of an internally developed, proprietary selection methodology that looks for what Diana Oreck calls "spirit to serve" and "organizational fit." Without these two factors, says Oreck, "you're not going to be happy working here."

And at FRHI, the company whose hotel brands include Fairmont, Raffles, and Swissotel, they use "a variety of profiling/predictive tools depending on the role—whether they'll be working face-to-face with guests or behind the scenes in the heart of the house; whether they're interviewing for finance or the technical side or as senior leadership. This profiling is an inherent part of how we select," says Doug Carr, the executive director for distribution at FRHI. "I've seen organizations that will hire just about anyone and then wait to see who washes out on the job–but that approach leads to absolute carnage! Think how many guests are alienated during that process of deciding, on the job, whether or not a new employee is a fit. Or the resources wasted to train them when there was no chance they'd ever really work out."

If your organization isn't ready to engage Predictive Index (used by The Broadmoor), HUMANeX (used by Radisson and others), Gallup or Talent Plus (two others that are popular in the industry), or another customized selection partner to help you sort through applicants, it's still possible to be systematic. The first place to start building your selection system is to formalize what you're looking for. This is a good place to consider my classic, psychologically supported WETCO formula, which I recommend as a general selection tool for guest-facing positions. (Silly but effective tip: You'll always be able to remember my WETCO formula if you picture a big, wet dog standing outside PETCO.)[10]

Micah's "WETCO" List of Desirable Traits for Prospective Customer-Facing Employees:

+ **W**armth: the quality of simple human kindness

+ **E**mpathy: the ability to sense what another person is feeling

+ **T**eamwork: an inclination toward "Let's work together to make this happen" rather than "I'd rather do it all myself"

+ **C**onscientiousness: a propensity for keeping track of details, and an ability and willingness to follow through to completion

+ **O**ptimism: the ability to bounce back and to not internalize challenges

Danny Meyer uses a slightly different list, which he shares with us below. I'm not here to tell you which list is better—they're strikingly similar, actually—but I *will* point out that the otherwise unassailable Mr. Meyer has, unlike me, failed to make his formula spell anything acrostically except "OIWESI."

Danny Meyer's List of Traits That Make Up a
Prospective Employee's "Hospitality Quotient"

+ **O**ptimistic warmth: genuine kindness, thoughtfulness, and a sense that the glass is always at least half full

+ **I**ntelligence: not just "smarts," but an insatiable curiosity to learn for the sake of learning

+ **W**ork ethic: a natural tendency to do something as well as it can possibly be done

+ **E**mpathy: an awareness of, care for, and connection to how others feel and how your actions make others feel

+ **S**elf-awareness: an understanding of what makes you tick

+ **I**ntegrity: a natural inclination to be accountable for doing the right thing with honesty and superb judgment[11]

Now, knowing what you're looking for, how do you select for my WETCO or for Danny Meyer's OIWESI, or for any other list of desirable traits? Here are a few suggestions, still assuming you're doing this without the assistance of HUMANeX or Predictive Index or another similar partner.

Consider purchasing a program of diagnostic psychological profiling tools, being sure to consult with the vendor to determine the best choice from among what they offer. Then verify the applicability of your new tools as follows: Ask your very best employee(s) (or the employee[s] most similar to those you're hoping to select in the future) to be profiled. Then have a more average-achieving employee or employees also go through profiling. If the profiling tools used are able to distinguish between the two (i.e., the outstanding employee[s] show outstanding profile scores and your middle of the road employees' scores are appropriately middle of the road), then you have verified its basic utility.

Now, augment your rough-profiling instrument with some other common sense approaches:

- **Use behavioral-based interviewing.** To the extent that you give credence to traditional interviewing (see below for The Broadmoor's Ann Alba's skepticism, which I share, about interviews), ask a lot of "Tell me about a time that you _____"-type of questions and fewer "What are your strengths and weaknesses?" questions. You'll get a fuller picture of your applicant.

- **Pay attention to how the applicant treats existing employees.** Ann Alba, the Broadmoor's resident manager, says that long before they had their Predictive Index functionality in place, they used an approach that served them better than an overreliance on interviews. "I believe almost anyone can build themselves up for a good interview," she says. "I'm more interested in what I hear back from my team about how [the prospect] treated the garage attendant as they arrived on the property, how they treated the receptionist, how they interacted with the staff they passed in the hall, because that shows the true guest-service heart and how real it is in person." Danny Meyer agrees: During the "shadowing" that top applicants undertake before they're made permanent with the company, Meyer's interested in feedback from team members at all levels of the organization who encountered the applicant in this nearly real-life situation.[12]

DANNY MEYER'S STICK SHIFT THEORY

Even though it's crucial to select employees for desirable personality traits rather than only for their technical skills, once you've done that, you'll of course still need to develop these raw but promising recruits into highly skilled employees. And you'll need to do this before they ever represent your organization in front of customers. Otherwise, you're doing your customers, and your company, a huge disservice.

Danny Meyer: "I used to think that you could just hire people for their emotional skills—that if they had the six essential emotional skills that make up what we call the Hospitality Quotient, that's all it took. I've since learned the hard way that you can't unleash somebody's hospitality unless you have first completely drilled all the systems, the technical skills and know-how that are needed, to a point of excellence."

In other words, the wonderful, warm personality traits that are the reason you've hired your new employees aren't going to manifest themselves with customers until the training for skills is complete and has become second nature.

Meyer compares this to learning to drive a stick shift:

Here's one way to look at it that may resonate if you've ever tried to drive a stick shift car. I remember what it was like when I first learned how as a teenager back in St. Louis: Until I'd learned to be proficient at the basics, I didn't have any fun at all while I was driving. I wasn't switching the stations on the radio dial. I wasn't telling jokes to my friends. I wasn't pointing out the beautiful trees on the side of the road.

At that beginner's stage, I was "all systems all the time." But once I learned those systems—how to shift gears, how to find a sticking point when I was on a hill—I could get back to being myself and pick the best music for whoever was in the car, tell jokes with people, enjoy the scenery.

So even though the emotional skills that lead to hospitality are not really teachable, they are also not revealable until your employee has learned the systems, the technical side of getting the job done.

Principle 2:
Select from the Largest Possible Applicant Pool

Selecting the best available applicants sounds great, unless the pool from which you're drawing them is small or inferior. With a shallow pool, you may be forced to take, say, the entire top 10 percent of those who apply, but if you invest in energetic and continuous outreach and in deepening that pool, you can succeed in giving your organization the chance to select perhaps only the top 1 percent of applicants—the best of the best.

As Brad Black, President and CEO of HUMANeX, puts it, "The secret here is ABS: Always Be Scouting." Once you know how to do it, there's no reason you can't be recruiting, or at least screening, prospective employees 24 hours a day via what Black calls "a marriage of technology and science."

24/7 recruiting works like this: Have an initial screening tool (some 30 to 40 questions, for example) available in a format that doesn't need to be answered in person. Those who make it through this screening should be automatically invited to sign up for step two of the process: a telephone interview. This means that someone who is working two jobs at present and can only find the time at, say, 11 p.m. to apply, can receive serious, sincere interest from your company by 11:40 p.m. in the form of an invitation from your company to take the next step toward coming to work with you.

If you're doing your screening 24/7, and getting back to prospects in a timely manner, you'll be picking your best from a much deeper and wider pool than if you essentially recruited whenever it was convenient for you, rather than for the applicant. And this can make all the difference.

It's also powerful to involve your entire organization in scouting for the potential employees who are, or can grow into being, as successful as your best current employees. This is what Black calls the hunt for "another one like our best." Involving your entire organization in recruiting is beneficial once a selection is made as well. You can now involve your "recruiters," the employees who referred the new employees, in the orientation process so that new employees are essentially being brought on board by their friends.

In some cases, you can also benefit from geographically broadening your search. This is certainly true for The Broadmoor, whose enormous operation, employing more than 2,300 workers at high season, is situated in the relatively isolated town of Colorado Springs. "When we're searching for the best person, the best fit for our organization," says Calvin Banks, director of training, "we don't just look at Colorado Springs; we don't just look at Colorado; we don't just look at the United States; we look literally around the globe."

Principle 3:
Tell Employees What You Want from Them—
Because Otherwise, You'll Never Get It

It's not enough to recruit and select the best potential employees. Great service requires not only that you select employees properly but that you also unlock their optional, *discretionary* efforts—the stuff that's not spelled out in their job description and that they can consciously or unconsciously either withhold from, or share with, your organization.

I'm a smart person. You're clearly a smart person. (I know this, because you have superior taste in business books!) And the employees you hire will often be smart as well. But smart employees can have a knack for doing just enough work—or what looks like work—to keep their performance *just above* the level that would get them into disciplinary trouble or cause other obvious unpleasantness.

Presumably, though, you didn't hire them just to watch them apply their innate aptitude toward the pursuit of mediocrity. (Case in point: Every restaurant patron has encountered those waiters who've cultivated an uncanny ability to avoid the glances of guests who are trying to get their attention. And we've all seen, by the same token, those waiters who develop a total knack for noticing and attending to the most subtle attempts of diners to get their assistance. Believe me, these two waiter scenarios—call them "good waiter" and "bad waiter"—can be acted out by the very same employee, depending on your actions as a leader. The direction that every employee heads in, whether they use their powers for good or for mediocrity, is up to you.)

So how do you get what you want from a new employee? A good start is to make sure that your employees *know* what you want from them. The most scientifically selected employees aren't going to be worth much more than a random assortment who were hired for, say, the letter of the alphabet their name begins with—unless you are able to inspire and educate them in what you're looking for and why.

This is not the big "duh" that it sounds like. In fact, it's the key, or one of the keys, to unlocking the elective efforts that your employees can either contribute to your organization or keep to themselves. If employees think you want only what's in their job description, then you're—as my Canadian friends colorfully put it—hosed. But everything changes once employees understand what you really want. Most people would rather please their leader and their peers than thwart them. You just need to ask them clearly to provide what you're looking for to achieve your aspirations for your organization and for the employees working there.

So what are your ambitions and desires for your company, your property, or your department? Try to get them down on paper. And it shouldn't take much paper; vision statements that are lengthy, Latinate, or jargon-filled are especially prone to non-implementation. Here are some great ones that actually encourage meaningful action:

- At Mayo Clinic, it's "The needs of the patient come first." Seven short, simple words that make priorities very, very clear.

- At Four Seasons Hotels and Resorts, the central principle is essentially the Golden Rule: "In all our interactions with our guests, customers, business associates, and colleagues, we seek to deal with others as we would have them deal with us."

+ At Fairmont Hotels and Resorts, it's the evocative phrase, "Turning moments into memories for our guests."

+ At The Ritz-Carlton Hotel Company, it's a simple, elegant credo that begins: "The Ritz-Carlton is a place where the genuine care and comfort of our guests is our highest mission."

To me, these are spectacularly short and to-the-point expressions of purpose, but I understand that you may be skeptical that words on paper can ever make that much of an operational difference: You know as well as I do that even the most haphazard of institutions have vision and mission statements, and nobody really cares about them. This doesn't, however, demonstrate that the words don't matter; it only shows that a lot of what matters here is in the implementation.

Herve Humler, President and COO of The Ritz-Carlton Hotel Company, elaborated on this passionately with me:

I encounter executives from other companies sometimes who tell me, "Oh, yes. We have a mission statement—it's about four or five pages long. It's somewhere in the CEO's office, and accumulates a thicker layer of dust every year." The problem in these cases is that the vision or the mission of the company isn't shared with the employees! The executive attitude is that employees don't work to create excellence—they only work for a paycheck, so why involve them?

I disagree with this wholeheartedly—in fact, it makes me feel, in cases like this, that it's these CEOs who need to be reformed, more than their employees.

Here at The Ritz-Carlton, our concept of service is well-defined through our Gold Standards and thoroughly communicated through our daily lineup and continuous training, which are how we reenergize our Ladies and Gentlemen to serve our guests consistently.

Our principles are the absolute opposite of just being words on a piece of paper. They are brought to life by the employees. At The Ritz-Carlton, we have twelve service values and three steps of service, and each one of our 40,000 Ladies and Gentlemen know them. They learn our values during orientation, and the values are then reinforced every day of the year at lineup. We even provide them on a laminated card that each Lady and Gentleman has on their person for reference.

Similarly, at Four Seasons Hotels and Resorts, their Golden Rule-based mission statement, committing everyone in the organization to treating guests, employees, vendors, and all other stakeholders as they, themselves would choose to be treated, is impressed firmly on employees throughout the selection, onboarding, training, and reinforcement processes until it is unmistakably understood to be "the way things are done around here."

And at the Mayo Clinic, one of the premier healthcare organizations in the world, their single, central sentence, "The needs of the patient come first," is drilled into every employee–whether they're a surgeon or a housekeeper–from orientation onward. For a surgeon, the implications are profound: No matter how splendid my scalpel skills, I will be conferring with my colleagues in other "competing" disciplines to get the best care for this patient. For housekeeping staff, the implications are similarly profound. If a patient, or a patient's loved one, needs assistance, or if there is something else I can do to assist in health care outcomes or patient comfort, I will stop my assigned duties (for example, mopping the floor) and get help for that person.

Principle 4:
You Need a Meaningful Orientation Process

Orientation (or "onboarding") is a crucial time for new employees. They're a bit freaked out and unusually impressionable during those first days on the job. In this time of excitement and stress they're looking for something to hold on to, whether that's positive, negative, or neutral. So don't waste this moment, when they're almost putty in your hands, telling them the details of the break room or about the forms to fill out for taking leave.

Tell them instead about your vision, about what their purpose is as employees in your organization, about what truly matters in providing superior hospitality. Get this across now, in simple, practical terms, and save the details, the minutiae, for later.

Hyatt's recently-overhauled approach to onboarding is a good illustration of this. Mark Hoplamazian, the president and CEO of Hyatt Corp., overhauled his company's process after realizing that orientation was coming across to employees as "100 ways you can get fired at Hyatt," because it had been primarily designed by risk management rather than by caretakers of the Hyatt hospitality experience.

"My epiphany came after I spent time face-to-face with a frontline employee," Hoplamazian tells me. "She explained to me how her excitement for working at Hyatt dissolved quickly thanks to our old orientation program: In her first 48 hours on the job, she told me, she had learned mostly about how she could get fired! The onboarding/orientation program was all about compliance, policies, rules, and regulations, like it is at so many companies. And the result was that it had terrified her."

How did orientation, a key moment in this employee's relationship to her new company, get so twisted and counterproductive? The answer lies in whose perspective was considered when designing this program. "It was designed by, and viewed through the lens of, our legal department to suit the compliance purposes of our HR department," says Hoplamazian. "Which is not, sad to say, unusual in companies today."

After uncovering this, says Hoplamazian, "we went back and redesigned the entire orientation process. The entirety of the first day of onboarding is now about what we stand for, what it means to be part of the Hyatt family—viewed and presented from an *emotional* perspective. Not from a left-brain, commercial perspective, but from a right-brain experiential perspective."

Garrett Harker is a prominent Boston-area restaurateur whose stable of restaurants include Eastern Standard Kitchen & Drinks, Island Creek Oyster Bar, The Hawthorne, and Row 34. A two-time James Beard finalist (2014 and 2015), Harker spoke to me about the evolution of his thinking on orientation:

> *As a culture, we've tried to shift the messaging during orientation. Eight years ago, we looked at the orientation process as almost trial employment, where we reserved the right to decide during the process [if] it wasn't a good fit. But by doing this, we were sending a message to our new hires that "we love you, but conditionally." Now, we try to convey to new teammates from the beginning that we think they have unlimited potential and that they have the unconditional support of their new colleagues.*

At The Broadmoor, every employee goes through a day and a half of orientation devoted exclusively to The Broadmoor's central, philosophical principles, history, and culture before going on to any kind of skills-related training. Calvin Banks, Director of Training at The Broadmoor: "That initial day and a half is very thorough, stressing the 'Broadmoor 16' [the hotel's central sixteen principles] and especially the first line of our mission statement, which is 'above and beyond our guests' expectations,' the principles that we live by. Only after stressing and re-stressing the philosophical grounding of the hotel will employees go on to more specific types of divisional or departmental orientation. Only then, for example, do food and beverage employees go on to a more specific training titled 'Five Stars of Food and Beverage.'"

Banks goes on to say that even in this later stage, which is more specific and technical, everything that's taught is taught in relation to its ultimate purpose: "It's still about going above and beyond, but now you're going to learn the 'how' of it: how you can best contribute to going above and beyond our guest expectations in your division. How does a culinarian do that? How does a server accomplish that?"

SENIOR LEADERSHIP
SHOULD LEAD ORIENTATION

To ensure that orientation is successful, employees need to know that it's a priority in your organization. A great way to demonstrate this is by having a person in the highest leadership level possible, ideally the CEO, personally provide a talk at the orientation about values, beliefs, and purpose.

Sound impractical, even impossible? Consider this: Danny Meyer, who as CEO of the Union Square Hospitality Group is about as busy a restaurateur as you can find, does this for all of his incoming New York staff. To keep it manageable, he now groups these meetings to occur every forty-five days, but he wouldn't miss them for the world.

And here's the example that will remove any possible excuse you may have: Herve Humler personally opens the first day of orientation at each new Ritz-Carlton hotel and resort that opens worldwide, a tradition that was started by the founding COO and that has continued, without exception, to this day. So I say to any business leader, regardless of the size of the organization: unless your leg is broken or you have norovirus, get out of your office, stop reading my book, and go *talk* to your new employees. *They will only be new once.*

Principle 5:
Take an Integrated Approach to Employee Development

Scientific recruiting and selection of employees is only the start. In all things related to employees, you need to be systematic, including reviewing your talent for advancement.

A perfectly selected, newly arrived employee is what Brad Black of employee selection and development company HUMANeX calls a "redwood seed." Lack of light and water can kill that seed pretty quickly (or can cause that seed—and here I mutilate the metaphor—to wander over to more fertile ground at a different company). "You always have to start with the right talent," says Black, "but those seeds need to be planted and watered. If you're not developing your new employees, not coaching them, not planting them in a culture that allows employees to build great teams, then you're not going to maximize the talent of those newly selected 'seeds,' and they'll never grow." The result will be low engagement and high turnover: negative results that directly affect the guest experience.

For an example of what systematic employee development can look like, let's consider the framework that was famously developed during Black's earlier tenure at Stryker, the Fortune 500 medical technologies firm. With this system, procedures are put in place to ensure that there's a management discussion about each employee within a specified period (for example, every 90 days) to ensure they're progressing in relation to their potential and their desires for career growth. "If our objective is to help them reach their potential," says Black, "the best way to do this is with a system that prompts us to have a regularly scheduled [leadership] discussion about every employee and how they can advance toward their goals in the organization every ninety days. This is the most humane, the most inspiring, the smartest thing you can do to get the most out of, and for, your employees."

Another procedure to schedule regularly is an annual check-in with each employee, to ask about the year that has passed and where the

employee sees herself in the future. At these meetings as well, management should give employees feedback about their talents, as measured
empirically and objectively, so that whatever the employees' talents are,
you're helping them to grow.

At The Broadmoor, they take what they call a "whole person" view
of employees: they strive to never look at an individual as a "position," or
"position-filler." Calvin Banks, Broadmoor director of training: "When
you think of an individual as a whole person, you're not thinking of them
as a server, you're thinking of them as 'Jimmy.' Human beings, including
Jimmy, have things that happen in their life. They have kids, they go on
vacation, they have up days, down days, aspirations, desires, frustrations,
good things and bad things that are happening in their lives. If we understand the whole person, on days when Jimmy comes to work and seems
not the same, we can sit down, talk with him, and see how we can help."

The power of recruiting right, selecting right, onboarding right, and
developing right are impressive. I always get tickled when I hear the way
Brad Black puts this sentiment into words: if you do your job right in
recruiting, selection, and development, "employees are going to brag
about what it's like to be at your hotel or restaurant. Now your worst
problem will be that you have to buy another hotel or find another property to manage because you have so many great people under your wing.
As they say, you can never have too much talent; you just have to find
more opportunities."

Principle 6:
Employees Should Be Involved in Designing
How Their Work Is Carried Out

Employees need to have input into the design of, and leeway in the
performance of, their work. And you as an employer *need* them to have
this input and leeway; it's a phenomenal, self-supporting employee development technique.

The principles that have guided The Ritz-Carlton Hotel Company since its founding include the following unusual goal (the language used has changed only slightly over the years): *"To create pride and joy in the workplace, all employees have the right to be involved in the planning of work that affects them."*

Watching employee-directed work groups at a Ritz-Carlton can be an impressive sight, even if the work in question is something as commonplace as setting up banquet tables for breakfast service. Maybe this doesn't sound like much of a show, but to me the breakfast setup activities—silverware put in place just so, green cloth napkins laid flat on the table for just one moment before being rapidly folded into a shape sort of like an origami sailboat, a fleet of self-supporting origami green-cloth sailboats that quickly grows to be 150 strong—can give the impression of an outdoor ballet, with the steps of each task performed deliberately, not in a rush but not idling. There's an impression that the employees have enough time to get their work done, but not enough time to be wasting it. And the most interesting part of this show? The employees performing these movements and exercising their skills have no visible supervisor. This work is undirected, yet highly purposeful, and you'll rarely see anyone missing a step.

Erika, a frontline employee at The Ritz-Carlton hotel in Naples, Florida, was quick to talk with me about how this self-direction extends throughout the hotel and organization. "The Ritz-Carlton is a company lets me use my best judgment to make guests happy. That makes a huge difference in how much guests enjoy their day and, honestly, in how much I enjoy mine."

Hands-Off Management—Up to a Point

At Hyatt headquarters in Chicago, Hyatt president and CEO Mark Hoplamazian shared an example with me of the value Hyatt is finding in moving toward self-direction. Hoplamazian was working on-site with housekeepers at one of his local Chicago hotels (as part of a rotation he does to keep himself in touch with all parts of the Hyatt organization), a housekeeper working alongside him pointed out to him how her life was being made difficult by Hyatt's approach to scheduling shifts. By moving toward self-direction, Hyatt solved (or is in the process of solving—the work is still in a pilot phase) a problem that has challenged many companies. According to Hoplamazian, "she [the housekeeper] told me, "Every once in a while I need to stay home in the morning to take care of my grandchild because my daughter works. I find this very difficult to do because of the way our scheduling process works." I reported this back [to the leadership team], telling them that "we've got to go back to the drawing board and figure out ways for people to easily flex when they need to."

But, in fact, a redesign directed from on high by Hyatt management wasn't what was called for, continues Hoplamazian:

> Unbeknownst to me, at the same time that I had this experience, a colleague of ours was in another hotel here in Chicago. A similar question was raised by the housekeepers. My colleague's response was, "Sounds to me like you all could do a better job of figuring it out on your own. So why don't you get together and figure out how you would prefer to have the scheduling work, and we'll provide you with the tools to help you do that, including the technology so the system that can be accessed remotely rather than you having to be on-site." [The issue here is that if a housekeeper finishes a shift on a Tuesday and leaves the hotel, her circumstances may change before her shift on Wednesday, so coming back to the hotel to reschedule isn't really feasible.]
>
> We've started doing this, and the response so far from the local team has been phenomenal. I'm very optimistic that we'll be able to take this to scale so we can allow people to feel like they're more

in control of their work lives and truly have it work commercially. Which I think is the right way to do it. There's no reason the house-keeping department can't self-schedule. They don't need a superimposed way to do that.

Restaurateur Danny Meyer also feels it's important that a leader "strike the right balance between letting employees 'do their thing' and actively course-correcting" when you see them doing something that goes against your ultimate leadership vision. "The goal is to hire really talented people and provide them with riverbanks, but not tell them how to row the boat. As a leader, I need to make it clear that if you go over the riverbank, it's not going to work—to let them know the principles and expectations that matter to me beyond everything else. But within that, I want you to show me some strokes I never even knew existed! It's up to me to define my vision of the destination, but it's not up to me to take away their autonomy, which is what lets them be magical and to innovate along the way."

In business, we have a terrible tradition going back at least as far as Frederick Taylor (yes, the "Taylorism" Taylor) that jobs are tasks done by employees but designed by their so-called superiors. As our society has grown more specialized, this bias has increased in its intensity. It's important to push against this, to let your employees know *what* they need to get done (what the objectives of the company and of their position in the company are), but, where possible, avoid dictating *how* they should go about designing their day and carrying out their duties. If employees are only doing what they do because you spelled out every little detail, you haven't created a culture or a sustainable approach. A culture is a living thing powered by and maintained by the people who are allowed and encouraged to be, in a meaningful way, part of it.

GENERATIONS IN THE WORKFORCE

Generational conflict in the workplace has become a growth industry lately for consultants, speakers, and authors. But I'm doubtful that this industry's central premise—the idea that everyone in a generation acts essentially like everyone else in that generation, and that it's possible, therefore, to "generationally manage" your workforce—is the most useful way to view the people who work for you.

Here's an alternative view of your workforce: Although there are, *on average,* differences between generations, they are dwarfed by the sharper distinctions you'll find between individual human beings. And individual human beings, rather than generations, are what make up a workforce. Doug Carr of FRHI (Fairmont–Raffles–Swissotel) speaks eloquently to this point:

> *For a hospitality organization to go out and say "millennials are this way" or "Gen Xs are like this" is too broad-brushed. Across all three of our brands—Raffles, Fairmont, and Swissotel—we stick to the approach of "Select the best," based on the characteristics we feel are best for the position. We don't muddy the waters by saying "when you're hiring a millennial, look for X," because, whether you're 22 years old or you're 50 years old, if it's in you to give heartfelt service, we want you working here. Psychologically, all such high performers, according to the methodology we use in collaboration with Gallup, are going to have very similar profiling characteristics.*

In regard to your younger employees: I take exception to the very vocal chorus that's been ranting about "kids these days," young employees who, so the silly talk goes, "expect medals for just showing up." Not only am I not interested in piling on, I don't think "kids these days" are deserving of any such pile-on. Millennial employees represent the best-educated (the most schooling, the highest SAT scores with computer coding and other advanced skills learned as early as middle school) and most thoughtfully-raised (more about that below) cohort in history. And, regardless of whether you agree with this assessment, you'd best get used to these younger workers; it's predicted that by 2025 three quarters of workers globally will be millennials.[13]

Having said this, it's true that different generations tend to bring different expectations to the workplace, and that there's value in understanding these expectations and fulfilling them to the best of your ability as an employer. As far as millennials in particular are concerned, here are some of these employee expectations, with suggestions for how to address them.

1. They want to share responsibility—so find ways to let them. Millennials, in many cases, have grown up under a style of parenting that supported individual empowerment, where the kids were almost always included in family decision-making. Now, as they enter the early stages of their careers, millennial employees are often getting a bad rap for coming into the workforce with an immediate sense of entitlement. While that's a gross overgeneralization, it's fair to say that they want work that makes them feel like more than a cog in a massive machine. So as an employer, "try to create opportunities that give millennials the chance to take responsibility and find success on a micro level before they move on to larger roles," says Jay Coldren of EDITION Hotels. For example, continues Coldren, "Make one small team of employees responsible for handling the ordering and stocking and determination of par levels [the quantity an item needs to fall to trigger a reorder] of the office supplies. In a restaurant, a small team can be made responsible for ordering the wines, while others are deputized to handle the stocking and ordering of the service ware, and so forth. Offering up such areas of micro-responsibility will keep your new workers engaged outside of the normal scope of their day."

Millennials also may expect a timetable for career advancement that comes off as unrealistic to their managers; as one hospitality leader said off the record to me, "Great people are coming into our industry who are highly educated and who all want to be directors of everything immediately." The most successful response to this is a simple one: compromise. Make it clear that advancement isn't possible on the millennial's idealized schedule, but that if they make a commitment to their current position and department that may seem long to them (yet is shorter than the previous norm in your company), they will be rewarded with additional opportunities for growth on a timetable that they can depend on.

2. Support their desire for work/life balance. Members of this generation are notable for their unwillingness to sacrifice their off-hours time or to make other lifestyle compromises in return for financial compensation. It's been argued[14] that millennials' inclination to think this way relates to their having watched their boomer parents delay happiness in return for career advancement, a worldview they're not willing to buy into for themselves. Regardless of the origins of this attitude, it needs to be taken into consideration by employers today.

Shelley Meszoly, Regional Director of Sales and Marketing at Fairmont Southampton (Bermuda), tells me:

> My younger staff will work their rear ends off for me when they're here, but they're also all about having their nights and weekends entirely free and clear.
>
> Work-life balance is incredibly important to these young people, as it should be, but the challenge is that working in the hospitality industry is in many ways a lifestyle—complete with frequent changes of venue and a round the clock customer base—that can clash with this goal.

There's no silver bullet solution here that I'm aware of. Humane scheduling is a challenging question that has been stumping even mighty Starbucks, which, after the *New York Times* shined a light on the issue, has committed to a company-wide goal of coming up with more compassionate approaches to work schedules. A start is to accept that this generation's desire for work-life balance is admirable and that any scheduling solutions that attain this will also benefit your overall workforce; the desire to have time for a life outside of work is not exclusive to any one generation.

3. Let them work for an ethical organization—by being one. Just like millennial customers, millennial employees (and potential employees) are concerned with organizational ethics and social responsibility. The extent to which you can satisfy these concerns will determine a significant part of your success in recruiting and retaining your pick of employees.

Doug Carr, again:

[In our recruiting], we work very closely with schools such as Cornell's School of Hospitality. The students who've been coming out of university for several years now are very focused on the social responsibility profile of any organization they're considering working for. They want to know your company's stance on the environment, on community involvement and social responsibility, whether your company wins awards for its eco-tourism or green lodging. All of this plays a large role in whether or not they're interested in coming to work for you.

4. They're hungry for feedback. So give it to them. This generation has received extensive adult feedback throughout their earlier years; they've often had close involvement from parents in their education and close support and encouragement from teachers and mentors at school. The contrast can be jarring when they arrive at their first professional position and suddenly have nobody who's interested in telling them how they're doing. One recently hired millennial told me, "This was the first time in my life that nobody cared about the quality of my work–or if they actually did care, I couldn't tell. The quality of my work could be great, or just okay; the response I received was the same either way."

The solution here is obvious and is an organizational win regardless of generation: Provide more input. Not just via formal, periodic performance reviews but through informal responses daily or weekly. Your employees will appreciate this, and you'll get more out of them to boot.

"AND YOUR POINT IS"?

Key Principles from Chapter 3:
"People Are the Heart of Hospitality"

▶ Words that are often little more than a cliché in other industries—"People are our most important resource"—are undeniably true in the hospitality industry. A hospitality organization can't succeed until it learns to effectively recruit, retain, and develop its employees.

▶ You select ("select" is the term hospitality leaders prefer to "hire") the right employees by taking a systematic, scientific approach to finding new employees who have the personality traits necessary for hospitality. Powerful professional assessment/profiling tools exist that can help you do this. Alternatively, the WETCO formula is a good general selection formula that defines the traits necessary in prospective employees for customer-facing positions: warmth, empathy, teamwork, conscientiousness, optimism.

▶ "ABS"—Always Be Scouting. Selecting the best of a tiny pool of prospects isn't good enough. You should be enlarging that pool, by scouting around the clock and by involving your entire organization in scouting for potential employees.

▶ Even the most scientifically selected employees aren't going to be worth much to your organization unless you are able to inspire and educate them in what you want from them and why.

▶ Orientation ("Onboarding") is crucial, and should be focused on organizational vision and employee purpose rather than on minutiae. Tell new employees about your vision; explain to them their purpose as an employee in your organization; make it clear what truly matters in providing superior hospitality for your guests.

▶ Orientation is most successful if it is conducted with the hands-on involvement of the highest level of leadership, ideally the CEO.

▶ Develop a system and timeline for checking in regularly with employees about their aspirations and their growth in the organization.

▶ Employees have the right to be involved in work that affects them. Honoring this right to self-direction is an incredibly powerful employee development approach that allows you to create solutions you'd never have come up with on your own.

4

Building a Culture of Yes

Guest: How big is the lobster?
Waiter: How big would you *like* it to be?

—Overheard in the dining room at The Inn at Little Washington

he answer is yes! Now what is your question? In a superior hospitality organization everyone should be striving to say "yes" to the guest, rather than figuring out ways to say "no" or "Sorry, not my department," or "It doesn't work that way around here," or "Sadly, we cannot accommodate that request," or "If you call back in the morning, perhaps we'll be able to help you."

That you should strive to tell your guests "yes" might seem obvious, even self-evident. Yet a single misguided employee can easily find a dozen reasons, every single shift, to say "no" to their guests.

"What If Bobby Flay Stops By?"

I call this tendency to default to an answer of "no" the "What If Bobby Flay Stops By?" syndrome, after a Mother's Day encounter I had with a fearful and intransigent GM at a remote outpost of the Bobby's Burger Palace empire.

In this nearly empty restaurant, my request that the music be turned down a notch so that my wife could carry on a conversation across the table with our children was rejected by the GM with an "I can't do that. What if Bobby stops by, and the music's not set like he wants it?"

71

Let's consider the logic of this response for a moment. Here's how I see it: In the unlikely event that Chef Flay did find time, between receiving his new star on the Hollywood Walk of Fame and managing the unending excitement of his personal life, to stop by this frontier outpost of his empire, wouldn't he *praise* the GM for making an accommodation for his guests, rather than upbraid the GM for violating a standard?

But this isn't the message that is getting through to his troops. And that's a problem. It's important for a leader to make certain that the message of "always try to find a way to say 'yes' to a guest, even when I'm not there to approve it" gets through to your frontline employees. It's the only way that employees will be able to give their very best to their guests. And it can make all the difference in the world.

I admire the way that Virgin Hotels has set "yes" as a very visible default at this new hotel brand. The red phones throughout Virgin's flagship Chicago hotel, in each guest room and in the hallways, have just one cartoonishly simple button proclaiming, in huge red print, "YES!" Press this button and you'll find a Virgin employee on the other end ready to assist you with your issue, no matter what it is. (I tried this several times, with excellent results.)

Raul Leal, the CEO of Virgin Hotels, designed the phones for his hotels this way after a frustrating stay he'd had at a competing hotel brand. "Their guestroom phones had nine—literally nine—different icons on them: to call housekeeping, valet, bellman, doorman, and so forth. As a guest, I just wanted one button—and I wanted to know that the answer was 'yes' without having to fiddle around figuring out the right department to ask the right question in the right manner. So that one button is all we have now at Virgin Hotels. And the answer there is 'yes' even before you ask the question."

"Yes" is also set as the default at Garrett Harker's stable of Boston area restaurants. Here's a poignant story Harker shared with me about a time that his staff went to great lengths to be able to tell a customer "yes" when they could much more easily just have said "no."

TOM COLICCHIO: THE "YES" CULTURE HAS TO TRUMP THE CHEF CULTURE

"The dark side of being chef-centric is when it hardens into an attitude of 'We don't change anything; you can take it or leave it.' Maybe that can work for a few chefs and a few restaurants for a short time, but ultimately it's not the way to build a business. Instead, you need to have a staff and workplace where *no* isn't in the vocabulary, where every encounter starts with the idea of 'We're going to say *yes,* and we're going to make it happen' as opposed to 'I have to check with the kitchen.'

"When you have a kitchen that doesn't get this, that is stuck in the 'no substitutions' mindset, it's not going to work. Because when a waiter's forced to do the old 'Let me check with the kitchen' routine, it means that for however long it takes to get the answer from the kitchen, the guest is sitting at the table thinking, 'They're going to say no. They're going to say no, I know it!'

"The better approach is to make sure that everyone in the kitchen and everyone on the waitstaff understands that *everything* can be adapted. So because the ultimate answer is going to be yes, it's best to go ahead and say that "yes" immediately and then work with the kitchen to make it happen. You definitely don't want to have those scenes where the waiter gets to the kitchen, and the chef down there is having a bad night and tells the waiter: 'Get out of here. Leave me alone.' When that happens, I like to tell the chef, 'Okay, *you* go in the dining room now, and *you* tell the customer *no.*'

"Also, once your staff understands that, no matter what, the answer is going to be yes, they can start looking at all the creative ways that you can get to that "yes." When a customer says, 'I don't really want the broccoli raab that comes in this dish, can you substitute the peas?' it might mean that they want to try the peas, not that they have anything against broccoli raab. It's a very easy thing to say, "If you'd like to try the peas as well, we could do that," and bring them a side of peas, rather than modifying the kitchen's original intention.

"This kind of open attitude also helps us solve more problems on the spot and save ourselves grief in the long run. We try to project an open attitude that helps customers to understand that if there is a problem, we want to hear about it. This is for everyone's benefit; it's really hard for us if you leave unhappy and two days later write us a letter saying that the fish was salty or give us an unhappy Yelp review at 2:30 in the morning. We can't help out at that point! It's a lot better for everyone if customers feel comfortable complaining right away, if they feel like we really want to hear."

We had an upcoming wedding shower scheduled at ES [Harker's flagship restaurant, Eastern Standard Kitchen & Drinks]. Unfortunately, one of the bride's invited guests was suffering from a severe form of cancer that kept her from being able to eat solid food. The guest reached out to us before the shower and requested that we serve her what everyone else was having but that we "throw it in a blender." Rather than resorting to the blender, my staff met on their own accord and created an all-liquid menu for her to enjoy in tandem with the other guests.

The guest in question, the late Carolyn Grantham, later wrote on her blog about her experience at Harker's restaurant: "Turns out they [Eastern Standard] had separate meetings to decide on a special menu just for me," including, for starters, "an amazing chilled corn chowder that tasted as though they'd extracted essence of corn, fresh from the field, and poured it into a glass." Harker recalls: "It was one of the proudest moments of my career to know that my staff went above and beyond to help this woman have a truly enjoyable meal despite her situation—that they found a way to give her a hard-to-achieve but unequivocal 'yes.'"

THE "I'VE ALWAYS WANTED A PONY" TEST

Have you ever called your cable provider and suffered through a customer service conversation that's scripted and stilted all the way up to the last moment, when the agent hurriedly asks you: *"Is there anything else I can help you with today?"*

There's nothing intrinsically wrong with this "Is there anything else I can help you with?" question; it's a sensible one if meant sincerely. However, there's a cultural and leadership mismatch going on when a contact center agent is forced to ask this scripted question even though the agent's call is being timed, she's not empowered to help, and her supervisor is actually hoping the agent won't have to provide any additional help because that will diminish their call throughput for the day.

This mismatch between words and reality tends to tempt me, out of sheer cussedness, to want to respond, *"I've always wanted a pony."* I doubt this would go over well with a stressed, unempowered telecom customer service rep, so, of course, I don't torment her this way. However, I've playfully tried this on one or two companies that are known for empowered employees, and received some smart responses from a Georgia peach of a flight attendant on Southwest Airlines ("We're plumb out of ponies, bless your heart"), LL Bean, and a couple of other great providers. Here, though, is the winning response:

Concierge, Four Seasons Hotel, Austin, Texas:[15] "Is there anything else I can help you with?"

Micah: "I've always wanted a pony."

Concierge: "I'll work on that right away," followed by four printed pages, in color, of horses available within twenty-five miles for purchase, that she slipped under my door (the printouts, not the horses) within minutes, with an offer to pick up any that I fancied, assuming my credit card could hold the damage.

The Power of Anticipatory Customer Service

One of the most powerful forces in hospitality is what I call "anticipatory customer service": finding a "yes" to a question or request that the guest hasn't yet voiced or perhaps doesn't even understand enough to put into words. Anticipatory customer service is a highly effective way to increase guest loyalty and to turn guests into brand ambassadors who simply can't wait to spread the word about your establishment. And what a house-keeping employee did for my family at The Inn at Palmetto Bluff, a resort near Savannah on the banks of the May River, is one of the loveliest examples of anticipatory customer service I've ever encountered.

The employee, Tonya, works as a house attendant, the housekeeping department position formerly known as "houseman."[16] Tonya pulled up outside our cottage on the sprawling Palmetto Bluff campus in her golf cart, bringing supplies such as bottled water, towels, and sheets for the housekeepers working inside. Three Solomons—my young son and his young-at-heart parents—were out front of the cottage as our son strug-gled to stay vertical on the bicycle we had borrowed from the Inn. Tonya saw my son teetering atop a bike that he wasn't ready to handle and instantly tuned in to the trouble we were having. She announced, "Your boy needs a bike with wheels," by which she meant training wheels, and returned in five minutes bringing us a bike newly equipped with training wheels, accompanied by Angella, a manager from Palmetto Bluff's recre-ation department, whom Tonya had brought with her to ensure that our son got off to a successful start.

This act of anticipatory customer service enhanced the remainder of our time at The Inn at Palmetto Bluff by allowing our son, on his now appropriately equipped bicycle, to range all over the gorgeous trails of the property. It was, if not life-changing, at least vacation-changing.

Tonya didn't just make an extra effort. She made the *right* extra effort. She saw beyond her House Attendant function, making use of her innate knowledge of guests, and of kids, to address what our son needed that we hadn't even recognized ourselves. She also stepped outside of her reporting area (housekeeping) to bring in help from another department (Angella from recreation) to make sure we got on track.

"Yes" and Then Some: The Pursuit of Wow

Creating a wow experience—a "yes and then some" effort that goes well beyond fulfilling basic expectations—is a powerful way to turn the experience of a hotel stay or a restaurant visit into something unforgettable that will live on in a guest's memories, encouraging a guest not only to return but also to share their "wow experience" with the rest of the traveling public.

At The Ritz-Carlton, "we intentionally create wow stories," says Herve Humler, "with a goal of giving you something so special that you'll always remember it. When I say 'we' create these stories, it is our Ladies and Gentlemen, our frontline employees, who make this happen. They listen to the guest, and in response to what they hear, see, and sense, they create something that is meaningful and memorable to that particular customer."

Diana Oreck, VP of The Ritz-Carlton Leadership Center, chimes in: "Wow stories are important to any business because stories are emotional transportation. For us, they're powerful because they lead to folklore among our guests and, in the retelling at the hotels, among our employees as well. Service, at the end of the day, is all about making emotional connections, and there's no way to make a connection faster than through a powerful story."

So what, in practice, do these efforts actually look like? Let's look at two different types of "wow," both of which happened within the confines of Ritz-Carlton's Dove Mountain property outside of Tucson, Arizona.

In this first example, the story created for the guest is small in scale, a combination of fixing an issue and then doing something a little extra, unexpected, and perhaps even slightly off-kilter. The guest had complained to the front desk about some issue with her water before heading off to dinner. When she got back to the room, not only was the plumbing problem fixed, but, says Liam Doyle, the Dove Mountain GM, "there was a note from Scott in engineering apologizing for the problem, giving his direct phone number in case he could do anything further for them, and including, along with the note, a chocolate wrench. The guest, who sent a thank-you letter to Doyle, concluded that letter with, 'I laughed through every bite of chocolate.'" Doyle is quick to stress that the idea for the chocolate wrench didn't come from him or from another manager; the engineering department employees took it upon themselves to create this wow moment.

The second example from the same Dove Mountain property is much more elaborate. And again it didn't originate with Doyle or another manager, but with his frontline employees taking spontaneous and self-directed action without asking for permission from management. Last summer, a family with a two-year-old son spent a weekend at the resort. As these guests were packing up to leave for the airport, the mom realized her son had lost his favorite Thomas the Tank Engine toy. Flagging down two frontline Ritz-Carlton employees, Jessy Long and Nathan Cliff, the guest explained what was at stake since this Thomas toy was her little boy's favorite and the loss would be heartbreaking for him.

Employees Long and Cliff failed to locate the lost Thomas train, but realizing how much this mattered to the guests, agreed together that something must be done. After the guests left the property for their flight home, the two employees drove to a toy store and purchased an absolute dead ringer of the original train for the little boy. They then composed a note in longhand to the boy in the voice of Thomas the Tank Engine telling a sweet tale about the extended vacation the little locomotive had taken after being accidentally left behind. The account included adorable pictures of Thomas exploring the property, cooking in The Ritz-Carlton kitchen (wearing a miniature paper chef's toque on his head), and more. Four days after the disappearance of the original Thomas, his replacement arrived by FedEx, to the astonishment of the family, who now share the story at every chance they find.

Lisa Holladay, the vice president for global brand marketing at Ritz-Carlton, spoke with me about the business logic behind such elaborate efforts. "In the example of the little boy and his lost (and then sort of rescued) toy train, our hope is that the family is going to remember that experience forever, and through family legend the little boy will 'remember' it as well, which is our goal—to create indelible marks through the work we do at the property level."

How To Build Your Culture of Yes

Let's look at what it takes to build and sustain a "culture of yes" in all the variations of "yes" we've seen in this chapter:

Hire for "Yes" Potential

When Tonya (of training wheels fame) was selected to work at The Inn At Palmetto Bluff, she wasn't selected just for her water-carrying, towel-schlepping abilities, but for what is *inside* her: her natural affinity for people and service. And when you hire employees such as Tonya, who are naturally gifted with innate empathy, warmth, and enthusiasm for people, you're hiring a staff that is ideally suited to picking up on opportunities to create a meaningful difference to the guests whom they serve.

Onboard for Purpose

After Tonya was selected for her people-centric skills, her training started with a two-day onboarding that Montage Resorts, the company that manages The Inn at Palmetto Bluff, calls "Mores." This immersion introduces new employees to principles that encompass the essential purpose of employees in the Montage organization, including finding a way to avoid saying "no." This "Mores" onboarding is in a sense a two-day indoctrination into "yes," and it happens before any more mundane training (for example, how to tuck in a bed sheet) takes place and well before new employees like Tonya are sent out to serve even a single Montage guest.

Model a Spirit of "Yes"

As a leader, you have to be careful about what comes out of your mouth when employees are listening and how you behave when they are watching. If you yourself are constantly voicing versions of, "Sadly, we cannot accommodate that request," *of course* your employees will follow suit and find all sorts of opportunities themselves to not accommodate guests. I know a veteran operator in the restaurant industry who's prone to telling stories to her staff about the times in her long career when customers have taken advantage of her, the times when she's caught customers who were trying put one over on her, customers who've bounced checks or have tried to slip under (or over) the age limit to get meal discounts as a kid or a senior. If you find yourself going on like this about all the tough, hard-earned lessons you learned on the job about how twisted human nature really is, beware! Your employees will absorb and reflect this attitude.

By contrast, it sets an important example when leadership walks the "yes" walk. For example, in April 2015, the managers of many Starbucks stores instructed their employees to keep serving coffee, absolutely for free, after their registers simultaneously broke due to a software update glitch. Although costly, such incidents provide a powerful opportunity for leadership to demonstrate, "We are here to serve customers, not to inconvenience them. We're going to say 'yes' to our customers now and trust ourselves to figure out later how to make back the lost revenue."

Make It Clear to Employees that Best Practices Aren't Intended as Excuses to Say "No"

Building and maintaining standards is of great importance, as I discussed in chapter 2. But standards and "best practices" (a term that sounds immutable and Ten Commandments-esque, rather than created by normal, fallible human beings) can also become an excuse to say "no." Whether the standard is "Kids' hours in the pool end at 5 p.m." or "We

WHEN YOU HAVE TO SAY "NO," SOFTEN THAT "NO" WITH AN ALTERNATIVE "YES"

If you're a skeptical reader (and, believe me, I generally am myself), you may be wondering as you read this chapter whether this passion for "yes" can actually work in the real world. Specifically, you may be building scenarios in your mind in which the answer must, in fact, be "no." Take this one: Say you're working at a hotel—let's make it Virgin's Chicago hotel—when a guest calls down from their room and asks if the hotel's on-site diner, Miss Ricky's (named for what Richard Branson's mum still calls him), is open. Since Miss Ricky's does shut down briefly in the wee small hours [to evade Chicago's weird law against 24-hour restaurants], the answer has to be "no."

Nonetheless, there's no need to abandon the pursuit of yes; we just have to move to a corollary that works when faced with such situations, the corollary of "Never say 'no' without offering a 'yes' at the same time." Which means the response could be along these lines: "I'm sorry, but Miss Ricky's won't reopen until 6 a.m. However, I have a list here of classic diner fare that can be prepared 24/7 by our Commons Club Kitchen, and I can have your choice of items sent to your room, or I can bring them to the seating area just off the lobby if you prefer to have a tabletop to dine on."

Long story made short: Don't say the "no" without having a "yes" to offer in the same breath.

Even if you're giving a guest a definitively negative answer, there's almost always a way to soften the blow by saying, "That's an excellent idea; however, we have a method in place that we find works really well for us. May I go over it with you?" And when "no" is the final answer, offering an alternative solution and an apology makes it easier to accept: "I'm sorry, Mr. Jamison, although we are unable to ship for free all eight pieces of luggage to Madagascar that you forgot to take with you, would it help if we shipped the suitcase that contains your most essential items overnight to you at our expense?"

stop serving from the lunch menu at 3 p.m.," employees need to understand that these standards are guidelines devised with the goal of serving
guests, not of finding ways to *avoid* serving guests. For example, let's look
at that rule about kids' hours in the pool ending at 5 p.m. There's a reason
for this practice when your pool is located adjacent to your tranquil spa.
But if at 5 p.m. there are no other guests using the pool and spa and the
kids in question aren't noisy or disruptive, why shouldn't the hotel let
them swim? If rules of safety allow a departure from the standard guidelines (which is a very important caveat around water), the rules can be
temporarily adjusted.

Reinforce the Spirit of "Yes" with Your Daily Lineup

Strive to find an opportunity every single day and every single shift to
sharpen your organizational focus on providing a "yes" for your guests.
Without this intentional rededication, the reality will likely be exactly
the opposite: Every day and every shift will provide a chance for your
initially positive focus to blur as you endure the daily frustrations of
serving customers. That's why the Ritz-Carlton routine known as the
"daily lineup," that they have had in place for more than thirty years, is
so valuable.

Lineup as practiced at Ritz-Carlton is a brief daily huddle that
employees hold in small groups throughout the company at the same
time each day (actually, same *times*, as they have more than one). It
shouldn't be longer than 15 minutes, because if it's any longer than that,
"it's not a lineup, it's a meeting, and nobody needs another meeting in
their day," says Diana Oreck, Vice President of The Ritz-Carlton Leadership Center. Each lineup is devoted to a single aspect of service, for
example, Ritz-Carlton's Service Value #2, "I am always responsive to the
expressed and unexpressed wishes and needs of our guests" or #6, "I own
and immediately resolve guest problems."

These discussions make use of examples from encounters with a particular guest or situation. "The daily lineup is the most important vehicle

we have at Ritz-Carlton for keeping the culture alive," says Oreck. Every single day, 365 days a year, three times a day (because there are three different shifts), "we have our lineup and cover the twelve principles that are central to our service culture in rotation. If today we're talking about Service Value #1, 'I create Ritz-Carlton guests for life,' and you're the GM in Tokyo and I am the GM in New York, we can't go out of rotation. What's fascinating is that within 12 hours, first our Asian colleagues, then the Europeans, and then the Americans will be hearing the same message."

(By the way, it doesn't have to fall upon a manager or a trainer to lead the lineup. On the contrary, a different employee can lead the lineup each day, thereby learning and teaching at the same time.)

Now, as you read this you may be thinking, "We *already* have a lineup at my company." And it's true that a lot of hotels, restaurants, casinos, and other hospitality organizations have some semblance of a lineup, whether this is simply the chef or manager checking in with staff to make sure they know the specials and have a pad and paper before the evening rush begins. But that's not what I'm talking about here. I'm talking about something that tries to *distance* your staff from the technical part of doing their job and *refocus* them on loftier goals.

"It is my job, and the job of every leader in this organization," Herve Humler, the President and COO of The Ritz-Carlton Hotel Company, tells me, "to daily remind ourselves and those who work for us at The Ritz-Carlton that we are not in the business of selling hotel rooms or F&B. We are in the business of providing exceptional service." If they do that well, Humler says, the rest of their job is easy and they will by default sell rooms. And if they get these priorities backward, they won't. "[This] is the reason that we conduct lineup three times per day, every day, all over the world. We remind our Ladies and Gentlemen daily about what is important to our customers, in order to keep it alive throughout the company. Energizing a workforce has to be a daily commitment. We pledge to commit ourselves to deliver excellence to our guests every day. Not whenever we want, but always."

Another difference between Ritz-Carlton's daily lineup and the one you may be experiencing elsewhere? The Ritz-Carlton's executives and the individual hotels' GMs actually buy into it. It's the farthest thing from lip service. In fact, they have a daily lineup in The Ritz-Carlton executive offices (think about that!) in Chevy Chase, Maryland, which Humler and the other executives attend daily, except when Humler is onsite at one of their 90 properties. In that event, he attends the lineup *there*. Every single time.

Reward a Spirit of "Yes"

By "rewarding a spirit of 'yes,'" I'm not talking about a system of financial rewards and prizes. Employees are smart people, often smarter than their bosses, and most systems along those lines will be gamed faster than the boss can blink. What I mean is this: Take a look at how you react when an employee goes the extra mile for your guests. You can either express your disapproval by punishing them for what they did (because the extra assistance they provided to a guest took extra time and reduced their so-called productivity, etc.), or you can celebrate their actions, make them a hero, and "reward" them. The choice is yours, and it makes all the difference. Every Monday and Friday at every Ritz-Carlton hotel and resort, says VP Lisa Holladay, "we share a 'wow story' from one of our 90 properties so that every other property around the world hears something amazing that a hotel did for a guest [such as the story of Scott, the engineer with the chocolate wrench]. This inspires other Ladies and Gentlemen to find ways to do something similarly memorable for their guests, to say to themselves, 'You know what? That wasn't that difficult. I could do that too.'"

What happened as far as recognition for Tonya's kindness to my son at Montage Resorts' Inn Palmetto Bluff? David Smiley, director of guest services, tells me that the very morning after I told him about Tonya's special treatment of the Solomon crew, he used Tonya's service as the centerpiece of housekeeping's lineup discussion.

Empowerment: The Final, Essential Element

There's another element without which your efforts will quickly run aground. For Tonya at Palmetto Bluff to be able to leave her assigned housekeeping duties long enough to find us the right bike and assistance, or for Ritz-Carlton employees to be able to run to the store and pick up a Thomas train set, photograph it in a series of poses, and FedEx the train and photos to a guest without questioning or involvement from their boss, employee empowerment is a must.

Complete empowerment? Well, pretty darn close. Because employees can only do extraordinary acts on behalf of a guest if they have the breathing space that comes with on-the-job autonomy. At The Ritz-Carlton, in addition to providing the proper tools, training, and appropriate workload to support guest-centric decisions, the hotel company doesn't just allow, but *encourages* its employees, once they're fully trained and up to speed, to use up to a theoretical $2,000 per guest to solve a guest issue or improve a guest's stay.

The power of having this discretionary choice to spend up to $2,000 is a tool to empower and encourage employees to use their time, effort, and—when needed—the company's money to enhance the experience of any guest, not only for a guest who has encountered a service lapse, but also for a guest who is already having a tolerable time that can be turned into a "wow" time. This approach is both about solving problems and finding opportunities. Frontline Ritz-Carlton employees, says President and COO Humler, "have total power, and all the resources of our organization, to create these moments, these stories, on their own, without needing to ask permission, without needing to involve management or worry that they're going too far. The time spent creating these stories isn't time taken out of their job; this time spent *is* their job." Humler continues:

> *Empowerment is often manifested as the power of our employees to break away from the routine. This requires attention focused on seeking out the moments where a break from the routine brings*

value to the guest: if you are a server, you listen to the customer, and if he expresses a desire for something different from what you are currently doing now, you cater to it. If you are a [maintenance] engineer and you are painting the wall or changing a light bulb and a customer says, "I need to get to the airplane," you can stop what you're doing and say, "Sir, I am going to take you to the airplane."

The attitude I strive to get across to my employees is this: "You are not servants, because unlike a servant, I want you to be engaged with the customer—you have a brain, you have a heart, and I want you to use them." This is why we say, and have always said, that we are Ladies and Gentlemen serving Ladies and Gentlemen. We mean this. We believe in the power of recognition and empowerment leading to great employee engagement. And employee engagement is critical to guest engagement.

Can you imagine what you've just read about happening in your own organization? Having your company president tell employees that they need to get busy finding opportunities to do more work, on the clock, for your guests and to spend more of the company's money, where needed, to take care of them? This is a very powerful approach, and nowhere near as costly as you'd expect it to be.

On the "problem resolution" side of the empowerment equation, no employee has *ever* had to make use of their $2,000 in discretionary spending, because The Ritz-Carlton's problem-resolution training is so phenomenal that problems rarely escalate or need to be solved as uncreatively as just throwing money at the problem. But think of the boost to employment engagement, says Diana Oreck of The Ritz-Carlton's Leadership Center, when anybody—a housekeeper, a landscaper—"knows that we trust them so much that if they wanted to, they could spend $2,000 on the guest without retaliation." Plus, this empowerment smoothes over service glitches very effectively because it lets the employee deliver an immediate, unequivocal "yes." They don't have to deliver a "Well, I'm not sure, I need to ask," and then run to get the manager and make the poor guest who's *already* been inconvenienced wait some more while the manager considers the problem and proposed resolution. "The results we achieve through empowerment," says Oreck, "are tremendous. And it is a huge trust boost for our Ladies and Gentlemen that makes them feel truly valued. It's very, very powerful, and it's how we create so many guests for life."

On the "delight" side of the equation, this managerial openness to do what it takes, regardless of the cost, often leads to creative but inexpensive approaches like the Thomas the Tank Engine switcheroo, an effort that I estimate cost Ritz-Carlton all of maybe $50 (including postage), but required the kind of quick thinking, creativity, and desire to serve that total empowerment can create.

"We've been allowed, in a true sense, to be artists," says Oreck. "We are trying to paint this beautiful experience for you, and we've truly been given carte blanche." This is powerful for the guests and for the employees in terms of the value and trust they feel coming from their organization. "A subtext of this is many of our people come from either war-torn nations or extremely difficult backgrounds. They feel so proud that they have been selected by Ritz-Carlton, and then to have us reinforce all the time that you are a Lady or Gentleman serving Ladies and Gentlemen, with the empowerment to serve them as you determine they should be served—to them, this means they have really improved their station in life."

When Oreck talks to other companies about Ritz-Carlton's complete employee empowerment, "my audiences lose their color. They go pale with fright. But there's no way around it. Without it, none of this would work. The issue is not the money, yet the monetary discretion symbolizes to our Ladies and Gentlemen that they're entirely empowered to do whatever it takes for our guests. Most guests are just looking to feel that you truly care, that you're making an emotional connection. Which is incredibly important because we're no longer living in a transactional economy. What matters today is all about unique, memorable and personable experiences."

Liam Doyle, GM of The Ritz-Carlton Dove Mountain Resort, says the trick is to convince your employees to "stop thinking about empowerment as an add-on. Your *job* is to be empowered! I reinforce with them, starting at orientation and every single day after that, 'you don't have to ask me whether it's OK to do what you have in mind—your job here is to surprise and delight the guest.'"

(By the way, if discretionary spending of up to $2,000 per employee per guest sounds impossible in your context, then look to Wyndham, which permits compensation up to the value of one free night by frontline employees without management approval, or the examples set by Hampton Inn and Hilton Garden Inn, which are both known for similar approaches. And, of course, great restaurants at almost every price point empower their employees to fix, replace, or refund items without waiting on management to make the decision. The amount of money involved isn't the point; the instant, non-defensive, no-need-for-approval empowerment is.)

"YES" ON A BUDGET

The need for one type of "no," of course, can be caused by guests making requests that simply don't fall within the scope you've defined for your business. "The nice thing is that most of the time, the marketplace calibrates guest expectations," says Robin Baney, COO of Oxford Suites, a family owned, primarily limited service chain of suite hotels in the Western United States. In other words, she continues, "While guests may have *high* expectations, the *breadth* of expectations [in a limited service environment such as Oxford Suites] is limited and for the most part can be anticipated." To distinguish yourself in your target market depends in large part, Baney says, on "understanding what those expectations may be and learning to anticipate and respond to those expectations better than your competitors within the same market segment."

Diane MacPherson, who with her husband John owns and operates the Foster Harris House, a three star B&B in the Virginia countryside, tells me that "at a three star such as ours, people's expectations are rarely out of line. It's unlikely, for example, that I'll get a request for a 5 a.m. four-course breakfast or for a grilled cheese sandwich at midnight. Of course, when such things come up, we address them with good cheer and as much flexibility as we can offer,"—sometimes by collaborating with local vendors to get the request fulfilled—"but my feeling is that the four star inn across the street gets, appropriately, far more of these kinds of requests than we do." So the MacPhersons concentrate their "yes's," so to speak, "within the parameters of our business—making the kind of stay we offer here the absolute best, most intimate, most memory infused that we can." Part of why their setup works is because, she continues, "We have face-to-face interaction with each guest, so we're in tune to their needs and can sense when the situation calls for us to go above and beyond."

Of course, there are always guests whose expectations will fall far out of line from what you can offer. You can reduce the likelihood of this, however, through preemptive guest education. For example, Suzy Hankins owns and operates the Ant Street Inn, a diminutive B&B in Brenham, Texas. The Ant Street Inn consists of only fifteen rooms ("keys," in industry parlance), and each room is unique. For example, Room 209, "Memphis," features exposed-brick walls and a layout that is dominated by a hundred-year-old freight elevator smack dab in the middle of the room. All of which is great until a guest arrives and asks for an early check-in into "their" room. You see the problem? Ant Street Inn has limited staff and *very* limited inventory: an inventory of *one*, in fact, if you have reserved, say, "Memphis." Suzy and staff can't service a room until it is vacated, and therefore, they literally have no control over whether the room the arriving guest is trying to check into early will actually be available for that early check-in. Because of such realities at Ant Street, Suzy actively makes use of guest education as her best defense against such unattainable expectations: "We spend a lot of time on the phone and in the copy on our website essentially training our guest as to what a stay at Ant Street is like: what the positives are of this enchanting property and, at the same time, what our limitations are, so they are prepared when they get here. It solves a lot of problems and it results in much happier guests—and employees."

It Can't Be "Yes" for Guests and "No" for Employees

To build an effective "yes" culture, you can't play favorites. "The message has to be the same everywhere," says Max Zanardi, GM of The Ritz-Carlton Istanbul. "My credibility is based on the fact that I'm genuine. If I am only hospitable with my guests, then it's not three-dimensional any more. If I'm scrupulous about letting the guest pass first, I need to also be consistent about yielding the right of way to my colleagues. Or let's say you are in the hospitality business but you wouldn't give a great room to one of your employees staying in your hotel. Examples like this happen all the time, and it gets very confusing to employees. Turning on and turning off hospitality is so much harder and less effective than simply keeping it on all the time."

The Ritz-Carlton's VP of global marketing, Lisa Holladay, continues the thought:

> I have watched our general managers stand up for Ladies and Gentlemen over very high-profile, high-paying guests that were really not being appropriate. I watched them put our Ladies and Gentlemen first. I think that's the true power of this company, because I don't think you can have our Ladies and Gentlemen delivering the service level we want them to if we didn't have the type of culture we have internally.
>
> And the wow stories we're so famous for delivering for our customers? We also have wow stories that happen for other Ladies and Gentlemen. We're not famous for these because they're internal, but I hear many times that "the reason I stay with the brand [as an employee] is the way that other Ladies and Gentlemen help me. When my wife was coming through surgery, my friends stocked my fridge and helped me with the driving; my work colleagues are some of the most hospitable people in my personal life as well."

Steve Bartolin, chairman of The Broadmoor expresses similar sentiments:

> *"Our approach here is that we're all in this together. We treat every-*
> *body with dignity and respect no matter what your job title. That's*
> *something that is talked about daily throughout this organization*
> *and held as paramount." Calvin Banks, director of training, chimes*
> *in: "We're committed to applying our Broadmoor values to how we*
> *treat guests, and how we treat each other. We want to make sure*
> *that we take care of every employee, as well as every guest, every*
> *single time, that every employee, as well as every guest, is having a*
> *great time while they are here."*

At the risk of repeating myself: if you're going to be a great company, a company of "yes's" for your guests, you also need to be a great company for your employees. Yet we've all seen the corners cut, the abuses that take place in the rough and tumble world of business, inside and outside of hospitality. So please listen to me: I'm not asking you to adopt a high-minded attitude based on altruism (although I'm a fan of that as well), but because the goal of treating not just guests but employees well is a straightforward and powerful part of a business strategy. It needs to be intrinsic to any game plan for serving guests in a superior manner: it's not going to work unless you serve the people who serve the guests.

Isadore Sharp, founder and chairman of the Four Seasons Hotel Company, speaks to this point eloquently—so eloquently that I'm going to let him talk without interruption for a few paragraphs straight.[17]

> *The strategic decision that transformed Four Seasons was the deci-*
> *sion to make the quality of our service a competitive advantage and*
> *a distinguishing factor that would be recognized by the general*
> *public. That led to the next decision, which was that if we were to*
> *accomplish this goal, the only people who are capable of performing*
> *that task are the people who work in the hotel, from the low level to*

the high level. Everybody who worked in the hotel had to be able to give the customer a sense of a sincere level of service.

If we were asking them to perform at this high level, we had to make sure we gave them what they needed: what would these employees need to inspire them to treat customers this way? That's when we put in place a commitment to the Golden Rule: treating people with the dignity and respect that they're entitled to, creating a work environment would lead everybody to rise to their best self, and where everybody recognized their particular role in performing service at a superior level.

Was it challenging? Absolutely. When we first set out to determine how we were going to behave [in keeping with this new corporate commitment to the Golden Rule], there were many problems. We had people at the very senior level of this company who wouldn't abide by it, so I was personally having a very difficult time because I knew that if these senior employees weren't going to walk the talk, we would have to separate them from the company. Which is what we ended up doing: many senior people in this company were terminated because they would give the Golden Rule philosophy lip service rather than sincere attention.

It takes years of slow work creating a team that are consistent in their values, believe in the philosophy, and are prepared to do their work while following the ethical behavior the philosophy implies: do the right thing, making sure that you don't compromise on the principle in how you treat everybody—your vendors, your customers, your partners, and your tradespeople who work there.

This isn't something that can be accomplished by putting up a plaque or making a speech. It took work over many years—I would say a 15-year period. Today with a company of over 45,000 people, there's no doubt in anybody's mind that the Golden Rule has been the bedrock foundation that has allowed the company to be recognized for the quality of service that distinguishes us from our competitors.

TRACI DES JARDINS: PUSHING BACK AGAINST A "NARCISSISTIC" RESTAURANT CULTURE

Two-time James Beard Award-winning chef Traci Des Jardins finds the customer experience "disorienting" when she eats at some of today's trendiest restaurants—in spite of being indisputably a trendsetter herself. The problem, says the San Francisco restaurateur (and former Iron Chef and Top Chef Masters contestant) is a shift to a "narcissistic" model of dining and customer service.

> It's puzzling to me when I go out to dinner sometimes; it's certainly not the same sort of hospitality that I practice. Waitstaff come to the table and say, in essence, "Let me tell you how we do things here," even to the point of saying "this is how you're supposed to eat [a dish]"; it's not about "what kind of experience do you want to have?" but "this is the experience that we want you to have."

Des Jardins' puzzlement didn't surprise me, as her own hospitality approach is so palpably customer-centered. Des Jardins is not only a cooking wizard, as her awards and every biteful at her six restaurants prove (for example, the melt-in-your-mouth tapas at The Commissary, where Top Chef was recently staged and which *The San Francisco Chronicle* recently named one of San Francisco's Top 100 restaurants), she's also a stalwart of customer-centered hospitality.

> My philosophy has always been to teach the service staff in my restaurants to give the guest the experience that they want to have, rather than having it be all about the restaurant and the chef and what they want to project to you. Though it is important for what's unique about a chef and restaurant to shine, I think the experience should always be dictated by what the guest wants to eat and experience.

To pull this off, she says, "you have to listen well and be nimble"; customer desires range widely depending on the customer and the occasion. "They may be looking for a simple bite and a glass of wine or they may want to sit for six and a half hours and have an elaborate, multi-course experience. I feel that most of my restaurants can provide that range of experiences, and pulling this off is part of what makes our jobs fun."

Each of Des Jardins' six restaurants has its own service vibe, from her flagship of fine dining, Jardinière, to the semi-formal Commissary, to the casual Public House, to the quick-service Transit. But in all of them, she advocates and strives to deliver this flexibility, this attitude of "if we have it in house and can make it happen for the customer, we will."

This also extends to the choice of food preparation. Athough Des Jardins is known for her flavor choices and strong sourcing preferences, she doesn't override guest preferences. "We'll do everything we can to get the guest what they want. With no judgment! If somebody likes their meat well done, though that's not the way *I* cook my meat, I don't have any judgment about that request. Ditto on gluten and vegetarian preferences."

Not Just At Five Star Properties and Restaurants

I realize that this has been a five star-heavy chapter, and I don't want to give the impression that great service only happens at five star establishments. To the contrary, "yes" service happens at all price points and in all hospitality configurations. It occurs at basic Best Westerns and at Best Western Pluses (a doubly superlative moniker that my family affectionately shortens to "Bestest Westerns"), Hampton Inns, Waffle Houses, and IHOPS. As a family, we travel the country in our minivan with multiple dogs and kids, and these establishments truly are our friends. We've had Hampton Inn personnel jumpstart our minivan;

Oxford Suites (the wonderful, primarily two- to three-star hotels in the Pacific Northwest that I introduced earlier in this chapter) make sure our dogs had plenty of water; and IHOP restaurants take extraordinary care of our kids, making sure, for example, that their "hot" chocolate be served closer to lukewarm, so that no youngster gets a nasty burn—and taking care of this without us even needing to ask.

So I'd like to end with a final "yes" story that takes place at the two and a half-ish-star Hampton Inn in Solon, Ohio, where my family was taking a "hurrication" during Hurricane Sandy. I don't think we could have received better guest service at any price point or any star level, especially the afternoon when it turned out the staff was scheduled for a meeting in the intended-to-be-closed breakfast area, an area not intended to be used by guests except during breakfast and the evening nachos and hot dogs happy hour, but that had been essentially encamped by the Solomons for four days straight as we waited out the hurricane back home, playing board games and anything else that came to mind.

This small Hampton Inn had been planning to host an all-hands employee meeting on what turned out to be the fourth afternoon of our stay. Fair enough. But rather than ask us to keep to ourselves that afternoon, the GM called my wife that afternoon, explaining the situation and what they were going to do about it. The Longhorn Steakhouse next door had a relationship with the hotel, and the Hampton Inn was going to treat us all to a carnivorously delightful late lunch there, and accomplish the dual purpose of being able to hold her meeting and give us a much-needed treat during our relatively grim week.

No steaks in the world have ever tasted better, and it's become one of our favorite "hurrication" stories. And, yes, the dogs enjoyed the leftovers.

"AND YOUR POINT IS?"

Key Principles from Chapter 4:
Building a Culture of Yes

▶ Make sure that employees are striving to find ways to say "yes" to customers, rather than hiding behind policy and best practices. (Exceptions are security and privacy-related concerns that may make a request unsafe, illegal, or indiscreet to say "yes" to.)

▶ To take this one step farther, learn to find a "yes" to a question or request that the customer hasn't yet voiced or perhaps doesn't even understand enough to put into words. This is true anticipatory customer service, and is one of the most powerful forces in hospitality.

▶ Make sure that the message of "always try to find a way to say 'yes' to a customer, even when I'm not there to approve it" gets through to your employees, rather than a message of "if you are overly generous with a customer there will be trouble when I get back."

▶ A special kind of "yes" is the creation of "wow" moments for customers—moments that make them want to tell "wow" stories about you. This is a very powerful way to delight customers and to grow and sustain your business.

▶ Select (hire) for "yes." An employee gifted with innate empathy, warmth, and enthusiasm for people is ideally suited to picking up on discovering ways to create a meaningful difference for their guests.

▶ Onboard for "yes": At the very start of an employee's tenure, teach the principles that go much deeper than the teaching of technical skills and routine standards.

▶ Model and give voice to a spirit of "yes." In particular, as a leader, you have to be careful about what comes out of your mouth. Especially be sure to avoid telling war stories about customers who have gotten away with things in the past. Beware! Your employees will absorb and reflect this attitude if you do.

▶ At the start of every shift, in the fashion of The Ritz-Carlton Hotel Company's daily lineup, take time to focus/refocus your employees on providing a yes for your customers.

▶ Reward a spirit of "yes." You can either punish your employees for going the extra mile for your customers (because it takes extra time and reduces their so-called productivity), or you can make them the heroes in your organization (because of the value that "yes" brings to guests, and therefore to the organization). Choose this latter option.

5

Developing a Genuine Service Style

"You have to practice an awful lot to come across as
completely unscripted (but it's worth it)."
—SARA KEARNEY
Senior Vice President, Operations-Asia Pacific, Hyatt Corporation

Whether or not the *level* of service you provide is excellent, if your *style* of service delivery comes off as artificial or cookie cutter, you're not going to connect with today's guests. Guests today are looking for what they perceive as a genuine hospitality experience, and they're easily rubbed the wrong way by anything in the service experience that they perceive as insincere, stilted, or inauthentic.

To illustrate this point, let me tell you a story that reaches back more than thirty years. The Ritz-Carlton Hotel Company, as a global brand, was created in the early 1980s. Very quickly, Ritz-Carlton became a major force in revolutionizing the hospitality industry by standardizing employment selection criteria, facilities, and more. Now, as a luxury traveler, you could roam the world and be able to experience a consistent standard of service akin to what you had experienced at the last Ritz-Carlton where you stayed, thousands of miles previous.

At the same time, the leadership of The Ritz-Carlton standardized one more aspect of its operation: the language to be used by its employees. In retrospect, this may have been an overreach, though at the time and for two decades running, it seemed to be working. Here's what I wrote some years back about the origin of the famous Ritz-Carlton brand language:[18]

> *To help launch their Ritz-Carlton luxury hotel brand [the founding leadership] decided on a set of ideal phrases for use in conversation with customers, then trained employees to use those phrases. The frequent use of certain phrases helped unify their employees around a shared identity and contributed to a distinctive "Ritz style" that the public could easily recognize: phrases like "my pleasure," "right away," "certainly," and, a personal favorite, "we're fully committed tonight." (Translation: "We're booked solid, bub!") The list of words and phrases to be avoided included " folks," "hey," "you guys," and "Okay."*

But to customers, such prescribed language choices ultimately came to sound insincere, especially when they were parroted by employees in situations where they didn't fit. The Ritz-Carlton's signature phrase, "my pleasure," in particular became a prime candidate for overuse and misuse. While "it was my pleasure to visit with you during your stay, Mr. Jamison," sounds genuine, "It will be my pleasure to unclog your toilet," takes the conversation off the rails. To make it worse, other hospitality businesses began to mimic Ritz-Carlton, thinking that by saying "my pleasure" they were somehow providing Ritz-Carlton-level service. Soon, for $2.99, you could get a guaranteed "my pleasure" from the drive-through window at Chick-fil-A.

So in the mid-2000s, after twenty-plus years of success, The Ritz-Carlton Hotel Company started to notice some disturbing feedback on its surveys. Recalls Diana Oreck, the VP from The Ritz-Carlton Leadership Center, "At that time, we began to get some alarming feedback from guests who felt we were coming off as too robotic" due to the rigidity of The Ritz-Carlton's language choices, scripting, and other carefully prescribed aspects of their service encounters.

"The good thing about that scripting," continues The Ritz-Carlton's Lisa Holladay, "was that it ensured consistency across the board. Unfortunately, what we started to find was that the very consistency itself was coming across as formal and excessively traditional. It was no longer tracking well with a majority of consumers, and especially with our younger guests, who perceived it as inauthentic."

Not too long after receiving this feedback, The Ritz-Carlton took action. Starting in 2008, and continuing to today, Ritz-Carlton hotels have done away with the strictly-prescribed language choices and scripted phrases. Herve Humler, who serves today as Ritz-Carlton's current President and COO and was also a member of the founding Ritz-Carlton leadership team in 1983, comments:

> *We've become intentionally less formal over time. We focus now on authentic, unscripted conversation and interactions with the customer. In the early days when putting together this hotel company and growing it globally, we scripted almost everything. You'd hear "my pleasure" repeated everywhere you went in the hotel because that was part of the script. We have evolved from that today and now encourage our employees to be themselves. To conduct interactions with utmost respect and courtesy, but in a way that is natural to their personality and the warmth of their caring natures.*

As The Ritz-Carlton and others have found, developing an authentic guest-service style is a requirement for success with customers in today's economy. Customers today, and younger customers in particular, are turned off by anything stilted or overly formal when it comes to communication. Their gut reaction to such a service style, even when it's delivered by the most caring providers in hospitality, is usually going to be negative.

This is why, in most hospitality settings (an important exception being interactions with privacy, safety, or security implications), I suggest doing away with prescribed language and word-for-word scripts while retaining, as needed, a "punch list" of points that need to be covered in the course of a particular conversational situation. (For example, to effectively book a guest for a spa appointment, you will need to go over a list of preference questions with the guest.) This approach to customer interactions avoids running into customers' innate dislike of being read to from a script.

Instead of requiring employees to follow a script, the best thing an organization can do is teach its employees to deal with situations, both easy and difficult, by giving them the tools to recognize guest behaviors and situations and to respond appropriately and effectively. As Christopher Hunsberger, executive VP of HR and administration at Four Seasons Hotels and Resorts, puts it, "The things that matter can't be scripted. You can build scenarios for your staff, but you need to couple this with encouragement and training for your staff on how to read the customer and then do what's right and what's appropriate."

◆ ◆ ◆

However, even if you're going to stop providing scripts, you should still be laying down language and subject matter guidelines to ensure that customers are properly cared for. This is what I call "language engineering." Train your employees to tell their guests, "Our records indicate a balance of X" rather than saying "You owe us X"; and teach them to say "You're welcome" rather than "Yup" or "Uh huh," "No problem," "Not a problem," or "No worries." Train them to say "How may I help you?" rather than "What do you want?" and so forth. "There's a difference between requiring employees to recite a script on the one hand," says The Ritz-Carlton's Diana Oreck, and "asking them to use natural but refined language on the other. Phrases like 'Hey, dude,' 'Wassup,' 'Huh,' 'Folks, calm down'—we teach everyone here that these are still not acceptable, even though we've done away with scripting." Oreck offers an example of unscripted but effective service:

> *Consider the case, which comes up every day, of a guest wanting to know about one of our on-property restaurants. A lot of training goes into being ready for these guest inquiries: we teach that you*

need to internalize your knowledge of the restaurant and be ready to give your own spin in how you share information with the guest who's asking anything from hours of operation to what is good on the menu. You need to be prepared and to have briefed yourself on this and be ready to speak. But we're not going to give you a script to memorize and recite. You can speak informally, as long as it's not inelegant. Your take might even sound as informal as this: "Oh my gosh, the best plate at the Café Bistro is the calamari. Our chef is from Italy and is really at the top of her game."

(*Note:* This phrasing, even though not scripted, contains a Ritz-Carlton secret that I don't think they'll mind if I share with you. Every employee is expected to have enough knowledge of every on-site restaurant to be able to recommend a particular dish, side dish, dessert, or drink as something that's worth trying. At The Ritz-Carlton Dove Mountain, the doorman Jim saw me as I was setting out to find the resort's on-site burger bar and called out, "Mr. Solomon, when you get to Cayton's, you really should try the mint milkshake." (And he was right.)

Part of the value of a program of "language engineering," discouraging certain phrases and word choices and encouraging others, is this: The employees that you'll want to have working for you because of their natural flair for service, come from a wide variety of family backgrounds. Inarticulate families. Uneducated families. Hyper-educated, talking-down-their-noses-at-you families. Language engineering can help convert gifted employees from all backgrounds into staff with the skills to talk to customers in a way that is unlikely to offend, confuse, or irritate.

As restaurateur Danny Meyer puts it, "You can be an authentically, genuinely nice person and still suffer from a gap between how you are being perceived and how you think you are being perceived." Because of this, says Meyer, "I definitely have phrases that I ask people not to use" in his Union Square Hospitality Group stable of restaurants. The trick, he says, is to soften these prescriptions by stressing that "hospitality has to be a dialogue. It cannot be a monologue. If you say the same thing, the same way, to every single table, you're conducting a monologue. You're not appreciating that every table wants to be treated differently."

Patrick O'Connell at The Inn at Little Washington tells me that his managers make use of analogies when training dining room employees—for example, that the waitstaff are candidates running for political office or are being groomed for an ambassadorship. "We're not trying to turn you into something you're not, but we need to polish the rough surfaces so you sound comfortable and at home in this environment, speaking to these guests." The dining room is a kind of embassy, he tells them. "You'll be dealing with a broad spectrum of people and we don't want you to speak in an artificial way, yet we want you to choose your words as carefully and elegantly as possible, while still being true to who you are."

Sara Kearney from Hyatt once shared with me what has to be my favorite sound bite on this subject: "You have to practice an awful lot to come across as completely unscripted." She then elaborated on this, in the context of her Andaz Hotels, Hyatt's innovative line of boutique luxury properties: "While we don't script, we definitely do a lot of role-plays and a lot of dress rehearsals to help people understand their role in bringing the brand experience to life." Andaz tries hard, says Kearney, to hire people who display a lot of personality as applicants—so why would they want to train that personality right out of them starting the day they're hired? "If we like you, we love your personality—we feel a real connection with you. Why would we then give you a script, change your behavior, put you in a stuffy starched uniform, and essentially suck the life out of what we liked about you in the first place?"

Here's what Doug Carr, executive director for distribution at FRHI (Fairmont, Raffles, and Swissotel), has to say on the subject:

> For me, what hospitality **isn't** is formula or scripting. When you
> open the front door of your home, do you always say the same thing
> to every visitor you're welcoming in, or do you adjust and custom-
> ize it based on who they are? If it's a longtime friend, you might

say, "How the hell are ya?" but if it's a family with kids arriving, you're not going to use swear words. Hospitality requires this same ability to adjust, depending on the situation and the guest. Which means that the most valuable thing, other than hiring, is to provide employees with training and tips on how to find the factors that should lead them to adjust their approach. For just one simple example, if someone appears to be hard of hearing, what are some of the things you could do to make life easier for them? If someone has a limp or a hard time walking, maybe when you seat them at a table, don't take them to an area of the restaurant where they have to go up or down stairs, even if you've been instructed that 'the best practice is to seat the tables in section X first.'

An Eye-Level Style of Service

Your service style will mesh best with today's customers if you encourage employees to act more like peers of their customers, less like servants, and decidedly not in a servile manner. You want employees to project the attitude that "everyone is in this together, the server and the served." While, of course, hospitality employees should be courteously deferential and eager to please, today's travelers are more comfortable with the service staff being on par with the guests in many ways, rather than standing apart in a subservient manner.

This, in part, ties into a more egalitarian ethos that can be traced back to generational change and linked to today's recession-scarred zeitgeist. Whatever the reasons, the "tea at The Plaza" model of service, design, and atmosphere, the white-gloved, British- or French-accented, towel-over-the-arm approach, doesn't really resonate with today's guests (except, perhaps, if you're actually having tea at The Plaza, where such ceremony is in its own way authentic to the setting). Guests perceive it as too imperious and stifling, too mothball scented. "If we go back in time, the luxury market traditionally came with a sense of formality, of dress and mannerisms that were meant to represent a higher level of society,"

Isadore Sharp, founder and chairman of the Four Seasons Hotels and Resorts, tells me. "[Such] companies brought with them a connotation of formality, good manners, etiquette, etc. I look at service differently. I feel that you can still be a great host without all those trappings. You can still convey the same kind of hospitality of welcoming and making sure that guests are treated in a manner that is respectful. People who come into the hotel perfectly manicured and dressed to the nines should feel comfortable, as should the person with a baseball hat turned backward and a pair of jeans."

"We don't want an imitation of a waiter. We want the genuine article."

Even in the case of Patrick O'Connell's double Five Diamond Inn at Little Washington, where a meal for two will run in the mid three figures (and that's assuming that both guests are teetotalers!), one of the reasons it has thrived is that the staff pushes back against the preconceived notion of a "fancy" restaurant. "We actively work against this," says O'Connell, "at least where it feels false and insincere to us. So, for example, we attempt to use no French terminology here, because, number one, we're not a French restaurant, and number two, we want to ensure there's no level of intimidation or lack of clarity. If there's a French culinary term, we'll define it in English, whenever possible."

Nonetheless, O'Connell tells me with an amused twinkle, the new employees who come to his restaurant often haven't gotten this memo about how service style has changed. "Because we're perceived as a 'fancy' restaurant, otherwise-talented employees come to us and start putting on airs. Often if waiters arrive here after having worked at another restaurant, for the first hour or so they strut around with that towel over the arm, and I want to say to them, 'Which bad movie did you see? Was it from the fifties?' You don't need to do that here. What you do need to do is put people at ease, take care of people, and make people comfortable in how you act and in the language that you use. The 'French' or 'fancy' airs that might have been cool at your last gig aren't cool here, because they're silly and artificial. We don't want an imitation of a waiter. We want the genuine article."

Choosing Your Own Uniform

If you want to create a hospitality experience and style of customer service that puts both customers and employees at ease, put some thinking into how employees are required to dress. The most successful sartorial approach is, by and large, to encourage your customer-facing employees to dress in a more or less similar manner to your guests. This puts guests and employees at ease and will pay dividends down the road. Also, if you're able to give employees a *choice* about what they wear (while still providing them with appropriate boundaries) it can help employees feel even more at ease at work, which is exactly what you want if you're aiming for authentic, eye-to-eye communication.

Christopher Hunsberger from Four Seasons tells me that until just a few years ago, "every male associate in the hotel had to wear a tie, a carefully prescribed shirt, and so forth. But in a lot of our hotels these days, that's not true anymore. If you go to our hotel in Kona (Hawaii), you'll see that our general manager there, Robert, walks around the resort in a pair of shorts and a nice Hawaiian dress shirt, instead of a tie and a sport coat, as in his prior years at the hotel. We changed this to signal to our employees that we want them to be more relaxed in their exchanges with the customer."

To take this a bit further, consider the cutting-edge approach to wardrobe standards that Andaz Hotels has taken. At these innovative luxury hotels from Hyatt, employees select and purchase their own "uniforms" from the line of a local designer who has been chosen as representing the vibe of the hotel's surrounding community. Employees buy the clothes off the rack to fit their own shape and size and are reimbursed for the purchase.

The Andaz approach helps employees *look* genuine for guests and helps them *feel* genuine as they go about their duties. Sara Kearney from Hyatt, Andaz's parent company, elaborates: "Part of the reason we decided to do this is that oftentimes, when you try to buy uniforms for so many different shapes and sizes of employees, the uniforms you end up with may not feel right to an employee. But if employees are able to choose their own clothes, it becomes a positive part of their feeling on the job, that sense of '*I'm wearing my own clothes!*'"

A hotel GM (at a hotel that I probably shouldn't name) cracked me up when he shared with me his take on the subject of wardrobe standards:

> *It's so completely backward: We're asking employees to "be gen-uine," and then we're dressing them, in the case of doormen, like Napoleon! The doormen at nine out of ten hotels worldwide are told to wear uniforms identical to the ones in the Napoleonic museum in Paris, the historic museum of the French Army! And we're telling them, when they're all decked out like that, to be hospitable, gentle, genuine, authentic? It's a mismatch and a disconnect."*

Grooming Standards, Tats, and Piercings

At the end of 2014, Starbucks announced sweeping changes to its tattoo policy: Tattoos are now acceptable even for customer-facing employees (everywhere except on the employee's face). Previously, Starbucks employ-ees had to hide tattoos under long clothing, which, as you can imagine, made things uncomfortable during a long day working over hot steam. Piercing restrictions have also been liberalized. These rules now read as follows: "When it comes to earrings, it's small or moderately-sized and no more than two per ear. Yes to ear gauges, ideally no bigger than 10 mm, and a small nose stud is allowed (no septum or rings)."

To me, this makes sense. As with loosening of clothing and language standards, employees who are accepted, tattoos and all, are better able to deliver a genuine customer experience that connects with the customer. In other words, letting employees revel in their own style is a way to project how genuine you are as a brand to employees and to the customers they support. Customers today project their own personal style through their clothing choices, tattoos, and hairstyles, and by and large they're fine with your employees doing the same. As service designer Tim Miller, who was SVP of EDITION Hotels at the time, told me, "The way I see it, you should strive for a visible symbiosis between the people working at your establishment because it fits their lifestyle and the customers doing business with you because it fits *their* lifestyle."[19]

Another benefit of letting up on your wardrobe, grooming, and body art standards is even more important: employees with the potential to be great all share certain key personality traits, but what they *don't* share is a particular look. This is the reason that The Ritz-Carlton gave me when they announced a similar relaxation of grooming standards, including, for the first time, allowing visible tattoos. Diana Oreck at The Ritz-Carlton Leadership Center told me, "We just could no longer afford to lose talent because Ritz-Carlton wasn't allowing facial hair for men or dangly earrings for ladies. We had to evolve; we're all in a war for talent. Let me tell you, there was pushback from a lot of people internally on this change, but we decided we needed to move with the times because our employees and prospective employees have already done so."

Caveat: On the other hand, there are some global considerations

When you're a global brand you need to proceed with care with all this. Language, grooming, wardrobe, piercings, and tattoos are perceived differently in different parts of the world. For example, tattoos are a gang signifier in Japan, so if your hotel caters to Japanese guests, tread carefully.

THE TALENT YOU SAVE MAY BE YOUR OWN

Nick DeRosa, head doorman at the Fairmont Southampton in Bermuda, is one of the greatest front-of-house employees you'll ever meet. He finds you the moment you arrive at the resort, offering an incredible smile, an energetic and kindly manner, and a musical, lilting voice. "This is the Fairmont Southampton," he says to welcome you. "I have been awaiting your arrival. I will be your resource throughout your stay. This hotel is owned by Fairmont, but the front is managed by me. If you need anything, even if you don't think it is in my area of service, I am from the island and can tell you all about it." (If my quote isn't exact, forgive me—my notes have salt spray and Popsicle stains on them.)

DeRosa represents to me the epitome of the talent that can be lost through grooming and tattoo restrictions. DeRosa has a tattoo on his neck that reads "Nick" in such large print that his much smaller name badge serves pretty much as decoration rather than identification.

Based on an appearance checklist, DeRosa would hardly be the likeliest candidate to greet guests at a grand luxury hotel, yet Fairmont put him out front anyway, based on his personality and smile. This has proven to be a great personnel decision. Not only is his stellar performance valuable to guests in its own right, but he is also an inspiration to the employees he works with to up their own game. So I hold the example of DeRosa out to you and ask you this: Why lose the opportunity to hire great service people because they made a questionable (to you) stylistic choice earlier in their lives—or, perhaps, as recently as last night?

The Great Name Badge Divide

Hospitality professionals are divided on whether name badges are a good idea or not in today's hospitality environments. It's surprising to me how deep these divisions are and how confident both sides are that they're right and the other guys are wrong.

The reasons *in favor* of using employee name badges are pretty obvious:

- **Making it easy to start a conversation:** "We want to develop a relationship between our staff and guests," says Mark Harmon, chairman of the ultra-luxury Auberge Resorts. "You're making it awkward for the guest if they have to ask a staff member's name. I find that guests love it when they can easily spot, and remember, the names of our people."

- **Symmetry:** Employees now often know the names of even first-time guests from their loyalty cards, credit cards, boarding passes, LinkedIn profiles, Google searches. Why shouldn't guests in this environment know employee names as well?

- **Making reporting and problem solving easier, for both customers and managers:** I had an experience recently with a hotel in Sweden misplacing a package I'd left with them. The manager was only able to resolve the issue because I'd seen the name badge of the employee to whom I'd entrusted the package.

- **Credit where credit's due:** It's easier to tweet about good service if you can say, "Dave put a great swirl on my latte" than "The balding guy with the hipster facial hair put a great swirl on my latte."

- **Deterrence and accountability:** As an employee who's had a long day, wouldn't you be less likely to flip off (proverbially, at least) a customer if you were wearing a name badge? Name badges are the service equivalent of that fabulous "Did Not Wash Hands" sign above the restroom exit in the *Far Side* cartoon. They provide deterrence and instant accountability.

For all of these reasons, a healthy swath of service providers, including the recent convert Starbucks, have made the decision to require name badges or other identifiers (at Starbucks it's an embroidered apron) for their employees.

Yet some hospitality providers are going in the other direction, doing away with name badges altogether. For example, you won't find name tags in the following hospitality environments:

+ Andaz, the line of boutique luxury hotels from Hyatt

+ EDITION hotels, the innovative luxury partnership between Marriott and hotelier Ian Schrager

+ Capella and Solis, the ultra-luxury creations of storied hotelier Horst Schulze

This is quite a division of opinion and practice. So what gives? Here's what Hyatt's Sara Kearney says about their choice to not use name badges at their Andaz hotels in order to have less of a barrier between employee and guest: "We're trying to make you—the customer and also the employee—feel like you're in more of a peer-to-peer relationship."

Tim Miller echoes this sentiment when he says, "[EDITION employees] don't wear name tags because we want it to be similar to when you're at home and a friend stops by and stays with you for a couple of nights. We want to provide service in a less artificial way than would be implied by the dividing line of name badged employees and civilian-dressed guests."

Miller does, however, sound a cautionary note: "We do couple this with advice to our teams that we don't want them to be too familiar. There's a difference between being friendly and being familiar. We are there to delight our guests. It's not about crossing the 'familiarity line.'"

The concern here is that, like scripted language, name badges may both make trivial interactions easy and put a cap on the level of intimacy a customer is likely to achieve with an employee or the brand that employee represents. If you're handed the employee's first name with no effort on your part as a guest, you can converse with them with zero effort, but you probably won't get any further than that zero effort conversation. And there's no question that an environment adorned with name-badge employees looks more stilted, artificial, and less genuine than without them. Hotelier Tim Miller again: "We didn't want the stilted awkward-ness of 'look, I work here, I'm taking care of you because that's what it says on my badge I do.'"

And boy do employees, especially millennial employees, tend to hate name tags. (An irony here is that the right to wear a personal badge stating one's last name was a hard-won victory for travel-industry employees in a landmark case. For many years, the porters on George Pullman's rail-road, all of them African American men, were, in a breathtaking display of racism, universally referred to by passengers as "George" regardless of their actual name, leading them to demand and ultimately win the right to have name badges with their own last name on them.) The current feeling among employees I've interviewed is that a name badge tends to be used by their more obnoxious customers not just as a tool to strike up better conversation but as leverage that allows them to threaten trouble via Yelp, TripAdvisor, or a complaint to the manager.

In the end, I'm of two minds on the name badge issue. Or, more accurately, understanding the arguments on both sides, I take it on a case-by-case basis with my customer service consulting clients, taking into consideration the type of aesthetic my client company wants to convey, the attitudes of their existing employees, and the preferences (to the extent that I am able to determine them) of the company's present clientele and the kind of clientele that it's hoping to have in the future.

Relaxing Your Style Doesn't Mean Offering Slacker Service

As you move toward a less formal, less scripted service style, strive to make sure nobody in your organization gets confused into thinking that your new informality is synonymous with slacking on standards.

"Our service style varies from restaurant to restaurant," says Danny Meyer, whose foodservice empire ranges from the extremely casual Shake Shack to the trattoria Maialino to the decidedly fine dining Gramercy Tavern and beyond. "If you go to Blue Smoke, our barbecue restaurant, you will be handed a menu by the person who seated you. If you go to The Modern at the Museum of Modern Art, you may not see a menu until your captain [headwaiter] has already taken an order for your aperitif. If you go to Shake Shack, you're going to stand in line and order from and pay a cashier. Then you'll be handed a buzzer that will let you know when your food is ready. But [the quality of the] hospitality we deliver isn't going to vary."

You Can't Achieve Authentic Service by Rewarding Conformity

If you're measuring and rewarding employee compliance, how can you expect authenticity? Mark Hoplamazian, Hyatt's president and CEO, is passionate on this point:

> We want to achieve authentic service, we want to enlist people to show up and be themselves, to engage in an empathetic way. But sometimes we've found ourselves organizing and measuring ourselves in ways that work directly against this. To give you one example, we used to send mystery shoppers into hotels and have them look for how closely we were sticking to the expected service sequences.

Did the person greet me by name? How many times have they used my name in the course of the check-in process? Did they talk to me about Passport [Hyatt's loyalty program]?

We used to have the shoppers collect this information and we'd feed it back to hotels as a metric. We've since discontinued this because we've realized that all we were measuring was degree of compliance, not degree of creativity or the other things that matter. We were trying, in effect, to measure some outdated version of perfection. And anyway, it's not about perfection. Authentic service beats out perfection every time.

Hoplamazian's observation applies throughout an organization. Creating and sustaining authentic service requires methodically going through everything you're doing. How you hire people. How you assess performance. How you compensate, encourage, coach, and develop your people: Are your processes, measurements, and rewards supporting, limiting, or even fighting against authentic engagement with your guests?

Creating a genuine service style isn't simple. There's a lot involved, in terms of both doing what works and undoing what doesn't. But it's a rewarding endeavor, and it's absolutely necessary if you want to connect with today's guests, as well as engage today's employee base.

"AND YOUR POINT IS?"

Key Principles from Chapter 5:
Developing a Genuine Service Style

▶ Guests today are looking for what feels to them like a genuine hospitality experience. So even if the *level* of service you provide is excellent, if your *style* of service comes off as cookie cutter, you're not going to connect with today's guests.

▶ When it comes to communication, customers today, especially younger customers, are turned off by anything stilted, overly formal, or obviously scripted.

▶ In most hospitality settings, consider doing away with prescribed language and word-for-word scripts, but retain a "punch list" of points that need to be covered in the course of a particular conversation. The exceptions are the security, safety, legal, or privacy-related concerns that may require verbatim scripting in certain situations.

▶ A better approach than scripting, in most situations, is to give employees the tools to recognize guest behaviors and situations and to respond appropriately and effectively.

▶ "Language engineering" means suggesting particular phrases and words to employees and discouraging the use of other words and phrases. This approach is more low key than scripting, yet allows an organization to take talented but verbally uninformed employees and convert them into employees with the skills needed to talk to customers in a way that is unlikely to offend, confuse, or irritate.

▶ To create a successful style of service for today's customers, it works to encourage your employees to act more like peers of their customers and less like servants.

▶ Today, by and large, customer-facing employees should dress in a manner that's similar to, or at least on the continuum of, how guests themselves dress. This puts both employees and guests at ease. This effect is further enhanced if you let employees have a *choice* in what they wear.

► Customers today project their own style through their clothing choices, tattoos, and hairstyles, and by and large they're fine with your employees doing the same.

► Employees with the potential to be great all share certain key personality traits, but what they *don't* share is a particular look. By being restrictive in how employees dress, how they style their hair, the tattoos and piercings they can display, and the jewelry they wear, you may be eliminating your chance to employ the greatest talent available today, for reasons that are literally only skin deep.

6

The Power of Authenticity

"You're not going to come to an EDITION Hotel and get a knockoff of anything. It's going to be the real deal."

—JAY COLDREN, Vice President, EDITION Hotels

Customers' quest for authenticity extends beyond the desire for a genuine style of service. In many other areas as well—architecture, design, furnishings, menu offerings, and more—guests today are looking for "the genuine article," searching for environments and atmospheres that feel timeless, original, or local.

To look at this another way, you can say they're eager to avoid what is explicitly fake. Today's customers are put off by all that seems phony, stuffy, or anachronistic. They want you to keep it classy—and I don't mean "klassy" with a "k."

To bring this into sharp, perhaps jarring, relief, let me share this excerpt from a rant by a young, sophisticated traveler:[20]

> *I ended up at a hotel recently that was everything about fancy that I hate. Marble pillars and gold leaf and every other possible ostentation that would make it absolutely clear to me that I was in a very, very fancy place. Part of what was off-putting was how car-centric it all was. As a pedestrian, it would've taken me half a mile just to get past the big* porte cochère *and the Rolls-Royces and Bentleys that they had fakey-parked out front and then continue down the long driveway to the sidewalk where I could actually take a walk.*

And the food was the last straw: completely nondescript—club sandwiches and such, nothing that made me feel I had arrived anywhere in particular—to the point where I just said to myself, "F*ck it, I'm going to go to sleep hungry." I checked out the next morning for a hotel down the street, one where I didn't feel out of place.

This young traveler was put off by the faux-luxurious hotel interior and the "fakey-parked" cars on display, and wasn't even remotely tempted by the "I could be anywhere" club sandwiches on the menu. Inauthentic cues like these are nonstarters with sophisticated travelers today because they come off as gaudy, sterile, artificial, and lacking in a sense of location.

So if these types of cues are turnoffs, what cues signal authenticity in a way that does appeal to today's guests? To some extent, what signals authenticity is something intrinsic to your brand: your origins, location, and unique features. And, certainly you're ahead of the game when you have a historically resonant property. A hotel such as the The Broadmoor in Colorado Springs, Colorado, in operation for nearly a hundred years and incorporating the personal hunting camp of their fabled Gold Rush era founder, Spencer Penrose, has a clear advantage here. So do hotels and restaurants located within historically significant buildings such as the Virgin Hotel in Chicago's neoclassical Old Dearborn Bank Building, which Virgin has faithfully restored to turn into the brand's flagship hotel. It is now complete with classic tile work (that had been formerly plastered over) and other decorative features from the original architects, Rapp and Rapp, who were best known for their historic, ornate movie palaces around the country.

There are other authenticity advantages a company either has or doesn't have, for example, a genuine founder or spokesperson who personifies the company such as Isadore Sharp who built Four Seasons from a single location motor hotel and is still chairman of the storied company, or Sir Richard Branson of Virgin. A historic (and true) company backstory can also serve this purpose, although you need be careful.

When you try to fake this, you risk looking ridiculous, à la Red Lobster suddenly pretending to have roots in Maine, a claim so patently false—Red Lobster didn't have a single restaurant in the state of Maine at the time—that I like to think it fooled nobody.)[21] But some genuine elements of a brand—the elements with which this book is concerned—can be consciously created as part of the overall guest experience you deliver through service, design, and programming.

In addition to authentic service style, including the avoidance of overly scripted interactions and maintaining an appropriate level of (in)formality, as was just covered in the last chapter, there's a lot more involved in coming off as authentic, including the cues you give your guests via their senses, which is the area I'd like to focus on first.

Visual, Tactile, and Sensory Clues

To come off as authentic to today's customers, design, materials, finishes, and furnishings need to look, and literally feel, different from the gilded, chandeliered ostentation of the past (unless your restaurant or hotel happens to be within an actual grand historic property, which, I would argue, has an authenticity all its own). Hospitality spaces that fit the new zeitgeist tend to not look as polished as their forebears do. There can be a preponderance of hemp, handmade tiles, and rough-hewn elements where the "hand" of the artisan still shows in the work—and human imperfections are a part of the appeal. In place of ostentation, they rely on proportion, good taste, uncluttered design, and the right materials: real materials that age well and create an impression of timelessness.[22]

Mark Harmon's Auberge Resorts operates some of the most acclaimed small luxury hotels in the United States and Latin America, including Auberge Du Soleil and Calistoga Ranch (both in Napa Valley), Esperanza (Cabo San Lucas, Mexico), Hacienda Alta Gracia (Costa Rica), and others. Yet despite the impressive VIP clientele and room rate that Auberge commands, Harmon is quick to tell me that "excessive spending is the opposite of our style of luxury. We rely on proportion, good taste, and great design in beautiful natural settings. I like to say that our resorts should 'look like they belong there' and have a strong sense of place. It's important to create a timeless look using real materials that look better with age." One of Harmon's California projects, for example, started with a design brief that said it would be "Napa barn meets San Francisco loft" with a playful, contemporary look and feel. "When we opened that hotel," says Harmon, "a lot of luxury was very gilded and marble and all that, and we went with concrete floors, simple cottages, an uncluttered feel intended to set guests at ease."

This approach, Harmon is quick to point out, is part of a greater whole: "The physical environment is part and parcel of what we are all about. We want to be warm and gracious in design *and* service. We don't have anybody running around in a black outfit trying to make you feel less chic than they are. There's no point in having a relaxing, lived-in style of design if you're not also about putting people at ease. And we are all about putting our guests at ease in their surroundings."

EDITION Hotels, the Marriott/Ian Schrager collaboration, is single-minded in its obsession with replacing the old and off-putting cues that feel inauthentic to today's sophisticated guests. "We've avoided and replaced negative markers we feel our guests are sensitive to," says Jay Coldren, VP of EDITION, "such as bad artwork, shoddy materials, garish lighting, and outmoded design. For example, our designers and creative partners populate each of our hotels with a unique collection of bespoke artworks commissioned for the hotel, as well as adding many other touches throughout the hotels that replace traditional luxury cues with a more sophisticated set of markers with a next-generation appeal."

What feels and doesn't feel genuine to a guest isn't simple to pin down or to pull off, and it shouldn't be executed simplistically. Some genuine experiences are authentically modern—think Stephen Starr's Morimoto restaurant in Philadelphia, sleek and streamlined—others are designed to take guests to another time and place. Gramercy Tavern in

New York's Flatiron District falls into this second category. Created by restaurateur Danny Meyer, Gramercy Tavern somehow feels like it has always been there. After a couple of glasses of wine and some of Gramercy Tavern's remarkable food, guests leave feeling as if they have been to an amazing roadside *relais* in the countryside, not a high-volume restaurant in the middle of the city. It's an illusion, of course, but it feels authentic.

Keith McNally's restaurants Balthazar and Pastis in New York City (and now London) focus on delivering a genuine French brasserie experience. But in the case of McNally's restaurants, these aren't *recreations* of a traditional French brasserie, they are *relocations* of traditional French brasseries. McNally's operational method is to buy a traditional operation in France and dismantle it, then rebuild it, piece by piece, in a strikingly different location.

The steps involved in creating "authenticity" can sometimes verge on the comical. When building out the Rosewood Inn of the Anasazi, a boutique hotel in downtown Santa Fe, the builders walked across the new, wide-beamed wooden floors in the restaurant with golf cleats and beat the floor with heavy chains before refinishing it, giving it a lived-in feeling, even on the day the hotel opened. In the same spirit of methodical madness, they took brand-new dining room chairs and threw them down a flight of steps a few times before refinishing them, to give them that patina of imperfection. But it all worked: the result is a hotel that feels like it has been there for generations.[23]

Finishes, well-worn wood, and bespoke artwork aren't the only interior factors that affect a guest's impressions. Look at your actual layout and flow as well. Andaz Hotels, the boutique brand from Hyatt that is in some ways a counterpart to Marriott's EDITION, has designed its public spaces with an emphasis on what Andaz calls a "barrier-free" environment, by which they mean an approach to design that reduces the number of barriers separating guests from staff, and dividing up its public space. (Note that in this context, "barrier-free" doesn't refer to removing barriers—thresholds, round doorknobs, and too narrow passageways, for example—that would prevent access to someone in a wheelchair or with other disabilities. This is another *very* important concept, but not what Andaz is talking about here.) For instance, at check-in, Andaz employees now stand or sit side by side with the guest or hold a handheld device in front of the guest where both can see it.

This side by side approach may seem like a minor tweak, but it made a big difference, according to Sara Kearney from Hyatt,

> [Andaz hotel employees] *started to see people's behaviors change immediately; it was really fascinating. The first week we implemented this, I parked myself in the London lobby to observe the effect. I remember watching the way people reacted when they realized that they were now side by side with the person who was serving them. It supported more of a peer-to-peer relationship. One of the funniest things that happened was that everybody wanted to see what was on the screen. In the past, it's always been that the front desk attendant looks at the guest, then looks at the screen, then looks at the guest again, then looks once again at the screen. But now, with the attendant holding an iPad and sitting side by side with the newly arrived guest, I would hear so many guests say, 'Can I see what you're looking at—what you know about me? What actually do you know about me? What's on that screen?' And, of course, we showed them.*"

I try not to interrupt interviewees when they're on a roll, but Sara's comment took me by surprise:

Micah: "You *did*? You showed it to them?"

Kearney: "Of course. The screen's facing you [the guest] now that the guest and employee are side by side: we've got either an iPad or some similar handheld device so the screen is facing outward. Our employee would answer, 'Look I don't actually know that much about you. Why don't you tell me more? Are there preferences we should put in your profile, to make sure we fulfill them for you, or is there anything more that we can do for you?'"

Micah: "But seriously, Sara, doesn't Hyatt have stuff in the guest profile that the guest wouldn't want a spouse to see or that Hyatt doesn't want the guest to see, like 'this lady's a piece of work'?"

Kearney: "No. Not really."

Micah: "C'mon, Sara."

Kearney: "At any rate, it wouldn't be on that first screen. In fact, what quickly became clear was that we really didn't know much about our guests, their preferences, background, and so forth, so this was a great way to engage the guest, to bring them closer to the brand and bring us closer to the guest. To me, this is a very powerful part of our new approach at Andaz."

Mark Harmon, CEO of Auberge Resorts, also believes that simple changes in layout and furnishings can support richer engagement with customers. "Customers have a visceral Pavlovian reaction when they walk up to a high desk with employees lined up behind it," he says. "They instantly feel like they're going to get hammered. So get your people out from behind the counter! If you have to have a desk, bring it down to a normal desk height and really engage the customer directly—go to the customer (instead of the other way around) and make it personal."[24]

Localization and Terroir

One of the most important signifiers of authenticity that guests look for is what can be called localization or *terroir*. This latter term is the French word for the convergence of factors—geography, climate, and so forth—that go into making a local wine, but I find it works in other contexts as well.[25] Lisa Holladay, the vice president for global brand marketing at Ritz-Carlton, says that when the company's first properties were being designed, thirty-plus years ago, they were intended to all look and feel similar: "The Ritz-Carlton hotel in Buckhead looked like Laguna Niguel, looked like Cancun, looked like Osaka. At the time, this fit with what luxury consumers wanted; it was reassuring and let you know ahead of time exactly what you were going to get when you chose The Ritz-Carlton brand."

Now, says Holladay, Ritz-Carlton takes the opposite approach. "If we're designing a brand-new property, for example our new one in Kyoto, we don't want it to look like a property that would be anywhere else in the world but Kyoto." For example, the lighting fixtures used throughout that Kyoto hotel are actually lanterns made by a tiny, local, ninth-generation family business. "It's a business that hand made the parasols the geishas use, which is, as you can imagine, a dying market. This company said, 'We need to reinvent ourselves.' Now, they take what used to be handmade parasols and turn them into beautiful lanterns. All of that history and heritage now informs a simple furnishings detail that for us localizes our Kyoto property."

Designer and architect David Rockwell's Rockwell Group strives to incorporate local culture into the hotel projects it undertakes, making use of "locally crafted design elements [that] can help connect guests to their surroundings." For example, with the Nobu Hotel at Caesars Palace in Las Vegas, a hotel based on the Nobu restaurant brand, the "challenge was to create public spaces, a restaurant, and guest rooms that reflect Chef Nobu's philosophy and also acknowledge the inherent dazzle of the Strip." So, Rockwell says, "We developed a design language that combines Nobu's rustic Japanese style with oversized elements and pops of color that reveal a touch of Vegas glamor."

The recent work that Rockwell has done for W Hotels also reflects his belief in incorporating the local environment. For the W Paris-Opera, "We took the idea of Paris being the City of Light and created a backlit perforated metal sculpture that weaves throughout this nineteenth century, Hausmann-style building [Hausmann was an architect significantly responsible for the iconic look of Paris], connecting all the hotel's public spaces." And at the W Singapore-Sentosa Cove, "We conceived a cosmopolitan oasis encompassing rosewood, orchids, and vivid colors that reflects and expresses the exotic beauty of the surrounding natural environment."

Another opportunity you have to offer a sense of localized authenticity is in the programming you provide to guests. Ritz-Carlton's Holladay tells me that at each of their properties, "We rely on our general managers to bring forward what's authentic about the property and its location through programming."

For example, at The Ritz-Carlton resort at Dove Mountain, which is in the middle of Arizona's Sonoran Desert, Ritz-Carlton offers programming for guests that includes trail riding in the unique desert landscape, addle addle lessons (addle addle is an ancient form of projecting arrows that predates the invention of bows), and a chance to study the prehistoric petroglyphs in the land trust property that lies behind the resort. The intention of this programming, Holladay says, is "to inspire you to feel like you couldn't possibly be anywhere else and have this particular experience." Which is quite a competitive advantage in hospitality: to be completely non-interchangeable in the memories you leave with your guest.

(Not that Ritz-Carlton claims to always get this right out of the starting gate. Diana Oreck, VP of The Ritz-Carlton Leadership Center, grimaces when she recounts the unfortunate story of how their South Beach, Miami, property once sported a harpist and tea service in the lobby, before the property came to its senses and replaced them with salsa music and authentic local cuisine.)

Is Localization the New Luxury?

"Money can buy you a bucket of caviar, if you're the kind of customer who chooses to spend your money that way," says Max Zanardi, the GM of The Ritz-Carlton Istanbul property. "But it can't buy you the luxury of having a tomato on your plate 15 minutes after it was on the vine." Unless, that is, you're Zanardi's guest at The Ritz-Carlton Istanbul, where you can get a still-breathing tomato on your plate fifteen minutes off the vine at their Bleu restaurant.

Here's how this magic trick came to be: Traditionally, the terrace pots just outside the restaurant have been replanted with flowers once a year. But recently, when it was time to choose the flowering varieties to plant, Zanardi asked, "Why do we always plant flowers? How about vegetables? What about herbs?" The result has been the conversion of the terrace garden to feature heirloom tomatoes and herbs in varieties that are local to the area. "We have received more goodwill and guest excitement from this than from just about anything we've ever done," says Zanardi. "It speaks to people's ideas of authentic luxury in our time."

FOUR SEASONS CONCIERGE ANDREAS RIPPEL: THE ESSENTIALS OF SUCCESS AS A CONCIERGE

Andreas Rippel is the Chef (Chief) Concierge at the San Francisco Four Seasons Hotel, a property that recently received its fourteenth straight Forbes Five Star rating. Rippel is a member of Les Clefs d'Or, the organization that represents concierges who are at the pinnacle of the profession, and he also has a presence in the changing world of technologically-assisted hospitality; he populated the "Four Seasons Recommends" module of the new Four Seasons app for his property. All of this made me want to speak with Rippel about his principles and techniques for providing superior hospitality to a demanding set of guests.

Micah Solomon: What makes someone a good fit for succeeding as a concierge?

Andreas Rippel: In my case, it was actually my manager at the Four Seasons Berlin [where Rippel was working in the restaurant] who saw the potential in me. Obviously, I didn't have the experience for it then. I didn't even really know what a concierge did, but my manager thought I had the interest in what guests are interested in: the cultural life, the museums, the exhibitions, and of course the restaurants—everything that a city has to offer.

I'm the kind of person who, whenever I go to a new town, I feel like an empty sponge. I can soak in all the information; it's just amazing to me. When my manager put it to me that this was a concierge's life, when he explained it that way to me, I thought, "Oh, this is a good fit for me." And it has been, for seventeen years so far.

Today, when I am hiring people with no concierge experience, it's all about the attitude, the approach, the smile, and how you interact with a person, because all the technical stuff, like how we do things on the computer, I can train a person in easily. Although, I cannot train a person in the knowledge of the city. That's something everyone has to do on their own. When I hire someone I'm telling someone, "You're going to be more or less married to your job for the first half a year because you need to get know the city. You need to be out and about and learn everything." We start with a one-mile radius around the hotel and then we spread out.

Solomon: Of course, in today's world, by default many people expect to get their information from crowdsourced, user-generated sites like TripAdvisor and Yelp. How does the traditional idea of an expert concierge—or, for that matter, any knowledgeable customer service or sales representative—fit into this new crowdsourced landscape?

Rippel: Concierges can contribute quite well in that context. One thing that has changed is that now, when guests come up to our desk for advice, they sometimes come with a list in hand and say, "I have this list of restaurants. I did some research, and here are five or six that looked good to me. Which one would you recommend?"

Which is a great place for us to come in. While Yelp can tell you what a restaurant was like for the person writing the review, my job here is to ask questions about the guest in front of me to find out how the restaurant will work out for *them*. To take a very simple example: I find out from them that they don't want a place that's too loud, and, well, I've been to those restaurants, and I know which ones are too loud. And this can make all the difference.

Solomon: What's the most central, basic, irrefutable wisdom you'd like to share when it comes to working with customers?

Rippel: One of my basic principles in working with customers is honesty. I just don't make things up; I won't pretend, for example, that I know something that I don't. If I did, in time it would come back to haunt me and would reflect poorly on Four Seasons and on me. A second principle, of course, is the one that is the bedrock of the entire Four Seasons philosophy: the Golden Rule. You treat someone as you would like to be treated.

This should be basic no matter where you are doing customer service or another customer-related function: working at the supermarket, or at the bank, or in retail, or at a Five Star hotel. The Golden Rule should be the expected way to behave, both with customers and with your co-workers.

Another essential is to find a way to be interested in the customer you're working with. Unfortunately, we don't only deal with positive input from customers, or positive situations. In such situations, being concerned and interested and empathetic go a long way. And it needs to be real; you cannot successfully fake it. So bring up from within yourself the part of you that can be open-minded and concerned and caring.

Solomon: Can you expand on this issue of working with frustrated, even obnoxious customers—not that you would ever describe your guests that way at Four Seasons, but still . . .

Rippel: Number one is listening, without feeding off the negative energy. Stay calm, and think to yourself, "I don't know what this person went through." They may have had a really bad day, there may have been issues with traveling, there were delays, something in the family or personally that they're dealing with. And it may be they simply are coming to the concierge to be listened to; that may not be the stated reason, but it can help a lot.

Apologize, regardless of if you're objectively at fault and, of course, try to help them as creatively as you can. The best thing is if you can turn the situation around. That's the best feeling in the world.

Believe it or not, I do like challenging guests. It's not exactly light-hearted fun, but it's certainly one of the things that keep my job interesting, even after all these years.

Solomon: Can you share a particular challenge you were able to transform with your customer service magic?

Rippel: A couple of years ago, we hosted a couple from the UK who were starting their honeymoon in San Francisco and were scheduled to go on to Hawaii. But a huge hurricane was threatening the Hawaiian Islands, so airline flights got canceled and hotels closed up shop. But I was able to book them a completely new honeymoon in one of our other resorts, where the weather was beautiful: our resort in Punta Mita [Mexico]. I changed all their flights, all their hotel reservations, and they were able to have their honeymoon in Punta Mita, which is a tropical resort that has the palm trees, the blue ocean, the snorkeling—pretty much everything they were looking for in Hawaii, but with a Mexican flavor.

It took a couple of challenging and intense hours to pull this off, but they were able to enjoy a honeymoon that otherwise would not have happened.

The Hyatt Brands Go Local

Of course, it won't be realistic in most hospitality environments to replace the terrace shrubbery with a garden of edible delights, nor is every hospitality venue going to have the advantages of a sprawling resort property like Dove Mountain's, where the localization can be accomplished on property. So you need to find ways to share the authentic and uniquely local aspects of the neighborhood with guests, which can be tricky, but is possible to accomplish at any price points and star levels. To take a few examples from Hyatt's rapidly expanding stable of brands: At

Hyatt House, the moderately priced extended-stay brand that caters to temporarily displaced guests, there's an impressive amount of "localization" information, meaning resources on the local community and how to navigate the area so the guest can settle in and feel more like a local.

Further up in room rate, Hyatt is now pushing the localization envelope with another brand, Centric, which opened in the summer of 2015. The concept of Centric is that it functions as what Hyatt calls an entryway to the destination. The hotel is intended to function as the hub of the guest's experience, connecting it to the best of what the local destination has to offer. Says Mark Hoplamazian, Hyatt's president and CEO, "It's about bringing the guest out into the neighborhood, being a conduit, a portal into the local community, sending people out to discover, as opposed to pulling things in. It's less hotel-centric and more destination-centric, a brand designed for people who are focused on discovering as much as possible about the locale they're visiting. The colleagues who are working in a given hotel generally live in those communities, and we involve these colleagues in helping our guests achieve a more eclectic, local, less institutional experience."

Taking on Airbnb

It's impossible, or at least foolish, to talk about localization without giving a nod to Airbnb and the enormous "sublet economy" phenomenon. Deserving of its own book, the sharing approach of Airbnb isn't something I can pretend to cover here in the detail it deserves. But I do want to make a few comments in the context of this chapter. Airbnb has authenticity via localization *nailed*. That you can get a true feeling of the local landscape is one of the key, hard to beat selling points of the Airbnb phenomenon: a feeling for the guest that they're truly getting immersed in the destination.

To firmly seat a guest in the neighborhood where they've arrived, every Airbnb property comes with an extremely local guide to the community, house, block, or neighborhood. Fred Dust, a partner at IDEO, a design firm that is renowned in the hospitality industry, says, "One of the great things about Airbnb is their local platform—how they curate the best things in neighborhoods. You get a neighborhood guide typically written by the person who lives in the house. It's literally, 'Here's the local scene, here are three restaurants I go to,' and so forth. It's one of the reasons why Airbnb has successfully expanded."

To compete against this, a more traditional hospitality organization has to obsessively focus on the positives it can offer that Airbnb never can. To fight back on the *terroir* front means to deploy your technology (for example, the new Four Seasons app has a locally-focused, personally curated "Four Seasons Recommends" section) and especially your human beings, your concierges and your staff in general, to localize a guest's stay even more than the most carefully written Airbnb guide can. The desire for authenticity, for living the life of a local, isn't going away. And it's time for hospitality organizations to realize the importance of this and to put it at the center of how they approach the guest experience today.

"AND YOUR POINT IS?"

Key Principles from Chapter 6:
The Power of Authenticity

▶ Customers' quest for authenticity extends beyond the desire for a genuine service style. In many other areas, such as architecture, design, furnishings, menu offerings, and more, they are looking for "the genuine article." They are searching for environments and atmospheres that feel timeless, original, or local. And they're turned off by anything that seems phony, stilted, plastic, or anachronistic.

▶ To some extent what creates authenticity is intrinsic to your brand: your origins, your backstory, your brand's founder or spokesperson. However, there is much that you can do to increase your brand's ability to authentically resonate with guests.

▶ Design, materials, finishes, and furnishings need to look and feel different from the gilded, chandeliered ostentation that used to mean luxury in the past. Instead, rely on proportion, good taste, uncluttered design, and the right materials, and aim for a strong sense of place. Use real materials that age well and create a feeling of timelessness that helps to set customers at ease.

▶ Authenticity includes the idea of localization, or *terroir*: being consonant with your locale and community in, for example, your foodservice offerings and décor.

▶ A significant opportunity to increase your localized authenticity is through the programming you provide to guests. An overall goal should be to inspire your guests to feel like they can't possibly be anywhere else and have this particular experience.

▶ Hotels, whether via concierges or via well-thought-out technology, need to find ways to share the truly authentic and local aspects of the neighborhood with their guests.

▶ The desire for localized authenticity, or "living the life of a local," isn't going away. It's time for hospitality organizations to realize the importance of this and put it at the center of how they approach the guest experience.

7

Moviemaking and Magic

"Experiences are the luxuries that customers today—
customers of all ages—are seeking."

—MARK HARMON, Chairman, Auberge Resorts

Maybe there should be a line on customer exit surveys for "magic." Absent that, we end up measuring what we *can* measure about the customer experience. We ask tidy, hospital-corners kinds of questions. Were you greeted promptly? Was your steak cooked to the proper temperature? Was your check calculated accurately? All of which is fine up to a point. The trouble comes when you delude yourself by imagining that customers will somehow logically tally up every aspect of working with your company and then dispassionately, "fairly," rate it.

This, of course, isn't how the customer mind, or the human mind for that matter, operates. Instead, a customer either decides that she enjoys being your customer or decides that she doesn't. Your challenge in business is to succeed in conceptualizing a state of enjoyment for your customers: to envision what "pleasure" or "comfort" or "my happy place" looks like for your customer and then, and only then, work on the individual pieces that will make up this whole.

A Movie Starring Your Customer

I suggest that you think of this approach as "directing a movie that stars your customer." Once you decide to direct such a movie, putting the customer, rather than your business—its processes, its org chart—in the starring role, you can get to work creating a tremendous, emotionally resonant customer experience.

Scenography

The Ritz-Carlton, in fact, explicitly embraces a cinematic, or at least theatrical metaphor, using an approach called "scenography" to solidify The Ritz-Carlton's relationship with its guests and to ensure their hotels live on in the memories that guests take home with them.

Scenography isn't about features, spec sheets, room upgrades, and other easily copied competitive advantages. It's about creating a feeling. That's the magic of it and the reason that it's hard for competitors to replicate.

Scenography involves creating a property-wide theme and supporting it with design elements, lighting, cast participation, and so forth. This overarching theme supports the specific hotel's or resort's "sense of place," its uniqueness, even its quirkiness. For example, The Ritz-Carlton Half Moon Bay, perched above the Pacific Ocean, has adopted a theme related to California wine and the property's oceanside location, a theme that is brought to life with candles, s'mores and/or wine around the fire pits, and a bagpiper who plays each night as the sun falls into the sea.

Or look at (and listen to) what's going on at Ritz-Carlton's Dove Mountain Resort in Arizona's Sonoran Desert. When sunset falls, guests having cocktails outside become gradually aware of distant modal melodies played on a wooden flute by a Native American musician who is perched on a hill some ways away from the hotel. The music echoes off the mountains, giving in a sense an auditory guide to the local landscape.

I'm breaking out these individual components for you so that you can see how a "whole" has been created and can be re-created. But if you ask the average Ritz-Carlton guest what they loved about their visit to Dove Mountain, by and large the answer is "it was great," not "the Native American flute player provided the perfect backdrop to our evening." If any of those scenography elements were less than stellar, the "movie" would be less wonderful as well—but you can't count on guests to recall the individual elements. According to Fred Dust from experience design firm IDEO, when a creative firm that was involved in the creation of scenography surveyed customers after the fact, it went something like this:

We would ask, "What was your experience like?" They'd tell us, "It was amazing!" So we'd follow up: "What made it amazing?" They would tell us, more often than not, "I don't know." So, we'd prompt: "Was it the bagpiper?" They'd reply, "Oh, yes, I forgot that." [Your author, incredulous, needed to break in here. How can someone forget a bagpiper? But Dust stood his ground.] *So what's fascinating is that people can have an amazing experience, feel (and later come back for) the general halo, but can't say, without very specific prompting, what made that experience amazing.*

Creativity Carries the Day

To succeed with scenography requires, beyond any other factor, creativity on the part of the hotel staff, a creativity that should involve the hotel's managers and the frontline employees if the program is to succeed. Rather than there being a checklist that can be referred to, like "Ten rules for successful scenography," the rules that matter are much more general, says Fred Dust from IDEO. Dust says the "rules, so to speak, come down to '#1: Leaders, be more creative! and #2: Empower your employees to be more creative as well.'"

Creativity is also required in avoiding a slavish, inflexible approach to implementation. After all, every guest is unique, and the concept of creating, directing, and supporting scenes needs to be modified, sometimes on the fly, based on the nature of the guest and the visit. For example, if you're not a drinker, you can count on Half Moon Bay's empathetic staff to pick up on this and not force their "red wine by the fire pit" part of the scenography down your throat.

Ditto for smaller touchpoints—individual *scenes*, if you will—each of which may require guest by guest adjustment. A stressed and jetlagged exec arriving at two in the morning needs one "scene" while leisurely lovers arriving midday need another, and so forth. Liam Doyle, GM of Dove Mountain, elaborates: "Scenography is the feeling and the story of the day. It goes on throughout the day, helping guests use the hotel—and the day, and the natural environment—as they like. It's not just the flashy stuff, though we do strive to have the feeling of the day come to a pinnacle, and for us at the Dove Mountain property, that's outside on the deck at 45 minutes before sunset, when we tell the myth of 'the spirit of adventure,' and the Native American flute player plays in the hills."

The Ritz-Carlton's commitment to scenography is at such a level that, every year, each individual hotel GM is required, in collaboration with his or her staff, to deliver three unique scenes as part of this scenography. And scenography is now required as part of each property's business plan, to lay out the scenes that they are going to be working on each year, with the dates for when they will be put into motion.

Aim for Enchantment

The overarching theme of the movie you create should vary depending on the nature of your business and, of course, on your particular guest. But if you're looking for a one-word review to summarize a successful customer experience, "enchanting" is a good adjective to aim for. You want to enchant your guests, to bring them under a spell, to transport them from the tedium of workaday life to a place that is, in some sense, magical.

This can be as simple as the way, at Five Guys Burgers and Fries, that customers (the nonallergic ones) are charmed by the throwback imagery of peanuts in brown bags, a very simple example of the way that successful restaurants have long understood that their job is to do more than feed people good, consistent food. This includes mainstream examples like Darden's Middle American-oriented chain Olive Garden Restaurant that famously strives to make the dining experience feel comfortably, vaguely "Italian" and provide a destination and experience outside the ordinary for its demographic of guests, and great restaurateurs like Jean-Georges Vongerichten who can create experiences so immersive, so experiential, that they feel like mini-vacations.

An evening at one of Jean-Georges' Spice Market restaurants, for instance, takes guests on a journey through India and Southeast Asia.

For those two hours, guests give themselves over to this carefully crafted fantasy and come away with an appreciation of another culture through its food and design signatures. Likewise, Thomas Keller's French Laundry is definitely not a laundromat in France, but it evokes the idyllic French countryside while remaining in the foothills of Northern California.

NEVER BREAK THE SPELL

Tom Colicchio feels that a great restaurant puts diners under a spell, "from the second someone makes that phone call, to their time in the dining room, with waitstaff moving through the dining room, actually *looking* at their tables, truly zoned in to what is happening in their station, to when the customers walk out of the restaurant and get in the cab." Colicchio says this spell is always at risk of being broken. "Even how you garnish the plates can disrupt the customer experience. And I think the kitchen sometimes doesn't get this because they're not out there [facing the customers]."

Colicchio tries to get the kitchen to understand this by saying, "Listen, just think about this. You're going out to dinner. You're spending a lot of money. Would *you* like that piece of salad on *your* plate?' They get it pretty quickly when it's put to them like that." The spell can also be broken by little awkward moments, "like having to track a waiter down and hail them in order to find the restroom," because the waitstaff wasn't attentive enough to the customer's more subtle attempts to get their attention. "And then, when they do, they're pointed down a long hallway" instead of having a waiter personally guide them there. "I even worry about the weather," says Colicchio. "If they have a great meal with us and step out of the restaurant and it's pouring, they're going to get soaked." Better, says Colicchio, is to walk them to the cab or, even give them a (branded, of course) umbrella, as Colicchio and his then-partner Danny Meyer did for years at Gramercy Tavern.

Enchantment can happen anywhere—even in the most serious of settings. Consider the Mayo Clinic, the integrated medicine mecca in the unlikely locale of Rochester, Minnesota. The Mayo organization has chosen to situate its children's cancer center right in the middle of one of its newest buildings—just off the lobby, in fact—because Mayo feels this makes the statement that their organization isn't going to hide, or hide from, this oft-dreaded ailment but is confronting it head on.[26] The lighting, as well, at Mayo's hospitals is a far cry from traditional hospitals' unnatural fluorescence. Ambient electric light subtly warms the walls, while the hospital's design incorporates outside light as well wherever possible.

Mayo also incorporates an extra layer of soundproofing in its building plans, mindful that experiences are formed from all five senses.[27] Through all the pain, fear, and uncertainty of a serious illness, this comfort and attention is in its own way enchanting.

The Drama's in the Honey

Salish Lodge, managed by Columbia Hospitality Group, is located in historic and scenic Snoqualmie, Washington, a lovely thirty-minute drive from Seattle. The Lodge (which you'll recognize as Great Northern Hotel, the setting for Twin Peaks) does perfectly well at getting things right on the checklist-type questions: they didn't ding our car in valet, they didn't miscalculate our check, and so forth.

But the reason we're already planning a return trip as a family? We'll go back for the magic. At Salish Lodge, the magic comes from a theatrical ritual involving their bees. No bees have snuck inside the airy but screened restaurant, thankfully. But there are hives of them on property that provide the honey for a tradition dating back to when the lodge first opened in the early 1900s.

The Salish Lodge ritual is called "honey from heaven," and here's what happens: The server comes to your table, her spoon raised high. From far above your plate, she lets the honey drip slowly, sensually off the spoon and down on to your breakfast biscuits.

Pouring from on high represents the neighboring waterfall that provides the backdrop to your meal. And it's magic. Customer centered magic.

Young (Or Not) and Adventurous

"Experiences are the luxuries that customers today—customers of all ages—are seeking," says veteran resort operator Mark Harmon of Auberge Resorts. "Whether they're young and looking for adventure and excitement, or older and checking off a bucket list, more and more customers are wanting to learn, experience, take part in something. They want to be able to come back and say, 'You know, I *did* that. I *participated* in this adventure. I did something that not everyone gets to do.' To give you just one example, we'll send guests off to go foraging with a chef at the market and come back and prepare a meal and meet the winemaker. We stage these unique experiences that people are after to create those special memories and moments that they're going to remember. That, to me, is the key direction our era is going, and we want to be right there in the middle of it."

Herve Humler of The Ritz-Carlton concurs. "Only eight, ten years ago, it was common for guests to be traveling around the globe, aiming to accumulate possessions: furs in Asia, porcelain in Europe, carpets in the Middle East or in India. But today, they travel for the experience, the engagement."

While Harmon and Humler are speaking to the experiential desires of all age ranges, the inclination appears to be especially pronounced among younger guests. In spite of being so famously tech oriented, millennials are hardly a bunch of cold, analytical drudges. As marketing consultant Andrew Jensen puts it, "It's a dangerous mistake to think of the millennial generation as hard-edged technocrats. On the contrary, this generation craves personal experiences."

Take business travel. Younger customers, including millennials, "tend to view business travel not as a necessary evil but as a perk and an opportunity to view the world," says Jay Coldren, VP of EDITION Hotels. The fact that many of these customers have yet to set down roots (recessions will do that to you!) means that they're less wedded to the notion of home and more open to travel as an adventure and opportunity. Simply put, they're looking for an experience when they travel, even if they're doing it on the company dime. Supporting this worldview by crafting an immersive, unforgettable experience can win you their business.

Jennifer Fox, president of Fairmont Hotels and Resorts: "[Our] research indicates that younger generations are looking for us to offer experiences and amenities that are engaging and educational, while also reflective of the destination," and, most of all, younger customers coming into the marketplace hope that "[we] will deliver an emotional narrative that resonates with them."

When dining out, more and more guests are looking for what's exotic, adventuresome, memorable, and new to explore during their dining experience. Especially among younger food enthusiasts, this has made "tastespotting" cuisine searches into a popular adventure, and created a cult following for food trucks (a concept evocative of dysentery for some of their elders).[28] You can find an intriguing riff on this desire for adventure at the Parker Meridian hotel in Manhattan. The ultra-sleek lobby features a high wall covered with a mysterious, plush gray curtain. Throughout the day there is a small neon sign at one corner of this curtain in the shape of a neon hamburger with an arrow. Guests who follow the arrow encounter a small door that leads them into a gritty, completely authentic twelve-seat burger joint. If you're lucky enough to score a booth, you'll find the names of couples carved into the simple wooden booths, ketchup and mustard squirt-bottles at each table, and press clippings randomly hung at odd angles on the walls. It is a 100 percent authentic, non-hotel, mom-and-pop burger joint in the middle of a five star hotel lobby. Genius.

Spicing Things Up with "Danger"

One interesting finding about today's customers is that many, primarily the younger set, even say they're willing "to encounter danger in pursuit of excitement,"[29] according to research by Barkley, an advertising agency that specializes in the subject. This may sound irrelevant to those of us who don't sell bungee cords, but try thinking of this idea of "danger" more broadly than actual risk to life or limb. "Embracing danger" isn't just about BASE jumping. It can mean the willingness of a customer to risk a trek to Voodoo Doughnut on a gritty corner in downtown Portland, aware that the line they'll face will likely wrap around the block and that the most popular varieties of donut—the ones with names so outrageously inappropriate (and/or shapes so anatomically accurate) that I can't even come close to printing or describing here—may be all sold out.

In a hospitality context, the seductive wildness of the setup at The Ranch at Emerald Valley in Colorado Springs is an example of answering the desire of customers for danger, or, at least, spine-tingling excitement. The Ranch at Emerald Valley, a group of cabins and main lodge 8,200 feet above sea level and only accessible by an ear-poppingly steep dirt road, as well as its sister property, Cloud Camp, yet another thousand feet up, are probably not what come to mind when you think of five star, five diamond accommodations. Yet these rustic cabins—which, it must be said, are airy, architect-designed, and impeccably maintained—are among the new, adrenaline-themed expansions of The Broadmoor property and marque.

Once you arrive high up the mountain at Emerald Valley Ranch, there's not a motor vehicle in sight, nor many other signs of which century you're in. After some impressively masculine "cowboy coffee" boiled atop the outdoor fire pit (later supplemented by a civilized, chef-cooked breakfast), the order of the day is a series of timeless outdoor pursuits like archery, fly fishing, hiking, or bouldering.

Emerald Valley Ranch and Cloud Camp are part of what The Broadmoor calls its Wilderness Experience, which also includes Broadmoor Fishing Camp on the Tarryall River (a restoration of seven miners' cabins and a lodge that date back to the late 1800s, situated on five miles of private waters).

Steve Bartolin, chairman of The Broadmoor, spoke with me about the philosophy behind the new Wilderness Experience additions.

All of these developments are out of the box as far as how luxury hospitality has traditionally been configured. We've expanded the boundaries of the typical resort experience experientially: we're creating these experiences that are uniquely Colorado, that have this adventure element, yet all tie into this mothership of The Broadmoor and our quality standards and service commitment level. It brings in a whole new element and attracts a whole new market—a cross-generational market—of guests who are interested in The Broadmoor but who are active, adventure-seeking, new-experience seeking.

What's Enchanting the First Time Can Flop as a Rerun

Humans, including the humans we call guests, will adapt to any situation, good or bad, over time. What's bad will eventually seem less bad (which is handy), but the good will eventually seem less good as well (which can pose a problem). In psychology, this is called the principle of hedonic adaptation.

This principle is important to consider as you work to maintain guest interest and engagement. Once you've initially succeeded in interesting your customers in your brand and succeeded in pleasing them with your customer experience and customer service, you need to work at *keeping* their interest by adding clues and cues to the plot, without taking away what they value, and you need to somehow pull this off without mistakenly removing what these returning guests value and expect, e.g., Indian flutes and twilight bagpipes, to pick two examples that I've mentioned.

Keeping it fresh isn't easy. Any initially meaningful element of your customer experience can start to grow stale over time. Service signatures, scripted interactions, and product offerings that delighted customers at first will be copied, replicated, and bastardized over time, often losing all or part of their originally intended meaning.

What's fabulous to a customer on a first visit one will likely be "fine but nothing new" on visit five. Consider the once fresh idea of printing a guest's name or business logo on the menu at a destination restaurant.

The first time a guest saw this personal touch, she was almost certainly impressed and amused. But when the restaurant tried the same trick on her yet again on her third or fourth visit, she was probably bored with it and ready for a new trick. There's a shelf life for such choreographed service practices and they'll need to be changed before they start to wear on the customer. Your guests are dynamic, aware people; the hospitality practices of your establishment should reflect this.

But change isn't an inherent positive, and it needs to be executed carefully. The goal of customer service and the customer experience isn't buzz, it's loyalty; it's the repeat business that keeps you alive. While it's true that customers seek innovation and freshness at the companies they frequent, if a company *only* invests in change, how can a customer remain loyal? What, after all, is left for them to be loyal to? This is the inherent tension between innovation and tradition, and it's hard to get the mix right. Patrick O'Connell of The Inn at Little Washington articulates this well: "Cultivating loyalty is a tricky business. It requires maintaining a rigorous level of consistency while constantly adding newness and a little surprise—freshening the guest experience without changing its core identity."

Don't Let Money Break the Spell of Enchantment

In his comedy, *The Dictator*, Sacha Baron Cohen of "Borat" and "Ali G" fame, plays a Middle Eastern tyrant modeled on Saddam Hussein. Arriving in New York and checking in to a sumptuous five star hotel, the dictator rants, "Twenty dollars a day for Internet . . . and they accuse *me* of being an international criminal?"

The comedian's point is dead on. No matter how extravagant the room rate, guests don't like to be hit with nickel and dime items such as Wi-Fi fees. In fact, JD Power's most recent North America Hotel Guest Satisfaction Index Study showed that guests surveyed registered a significant (65 points on a 1,000 point scale) reduction in satisfaction with hotels' costs and fees structure when the Wi-Fi wasn't free.[30]

And Wi-Fi fees are far from the only example of this. After a stay at an otherwise charming, boutiquey hotel in Canada, I came back from the experience still miffed about the eight-dollar bottles of Evian strategically scattered around the otherwise warm and welcoming hotel room.

It's not (not exactly, anyway) the cost involved that's so offensive. It's the interruption of the host/guest experience with mercantile, even mercenary, behavior. This kind of interruption, this breaking of the enchantment, is important to avoid. And it's why it's so much better if a hotel presents your room service meal without requiring the guest to sign for it. (What exactly is the benefit here of requiring a guest's signature before letting them dig in to their private meal? Is it to prevent her from claiming she never ate her room service dinner? Or that the bill is inaccurate? Or to try to milk another tip from the guest?)

It's why Virgin Hotels' "street prices" minibar (typical minibar goodies, but priced like they would be at a convenience store) and the in-room "Fresh Fridge" at Epiphany, the Joie de Vivre property in Palo Alto (a stylish SMEG-brand mini fridge creatively overstuffed with everything that is local, seasonal, and delicious by Patrick Kelly, Epiphany's Executive Chef, for one flat, reasonable price) are so smart. It's just not worth interrupting the hospitality experience and potentially alienating your guest to crassly seem to be grubbing for money at every stage of the journey.

It's also why handwritten, pencil-on-notepaper dinner checks, like those that the waiters write out and present at the end of a meal at Patrick O'Connell's Inn at Little Washington, are so lovely. They seem nearly apologetic, an implied attitude of "regrettably, we are required to charge you for this lovely evening we just spent together," rather than in any way suggesting that getting paid was *the point* of the whole evening.

O'Connell elaborates:

If a guest in a hospitality interchange feels that money is the first, foremost, and most significant component, they can't fully allow themselves to enjoy it. The trick is to be able to create the illusion of dispelling any financial transaction from taking place.

Now, of course, you have very significant economic concerns in this business; the trick is to be diligent in economizing wherever you possibly can, but to never, ever let it affect the experience of the guest. You need, actually, to go in the other direction when the guest is in front of you. If somebody wants more of something, we bring it. At times, somebody has said, 'Oh my, that was so good. I could eat two of them.' So, we bring them another! This attitude is absolutely central to a successful hospitality experience. I think it was best said in a journalist's review of a country house hotel. [Here, O'Connell quotes from memory] 'A great hotel is where the guest is having such a glorious time and they're chatting with the owner on the way out and they forget to ask for a bill because they feel as if they've just been entertained at his home and the host, the proprietor, not wanting to break the illusion, can't bring himself to present their bill.'

◆　◆　◆

Hospitality Included: Is It Time to Follow Danny Meyer's Lead and Get Rid of Tipping?

One common moment when money tends to break the spell of hospitality is when a restaurant guest is required to ponder and calculate how much to tip. But this tradition may be on its way out. Influential New York restaurateur Danny Meyer made waves recently by announcing that his Union Square Hospitality Group would be eliminating tipping at all of its restaurants, making it the first major US restaurant group to do this. (Some other notable players, including Ivar's, a landmark seafood restaurant with locations in and around Seattle, had made similar moves recently, and after Meyer's announcement, others of course followed suit.)

And Meyer is not equivocating. His restaurants won't even allow a line on checks for "additional gratuity," and they'll actively discourage those who feel any obligation in that direction. Instead, prices will be raised across the board to compensate, and all checks and menus will be marked as "Hospitality Included."

Meyer rolled out the new policy first at The Modern, his Michelin two star restaurant within The Museum of Modern Art, and the policy will soon become standard throughout Union Square Hospitality Group's foodservice empire, which ranges from trattoria Maialino to the fine-dining Gramercy Tavern and beyond.

Tipping is supposed to encourage good service. But does it?

Tipping, of course, is intended to encourage good service. And it arguably does, at least for a customer being waited on directly by the tipped employee. But it's far from a perfect system of reward. It provides potentially disproportionate compensation for a limited set of behaviors (the behaviors that are directly visible to the diner who signs the check), while ignoring the reality that superior service in a restaurant environment, as in any company in any industry, requires a broad range of seen and unseen assistance directly and indirectly to guests and to fellow employees.

The unseen actions that contribute to the dining experience and overall success of a restaurant, unfortunately, are compensated differently (or not at all, in the case of waitstaffs' required sidework). Heart of house employees, so central yet so invisible, are not tipped, and are often compensated more poorly than employees who are visible to the customer. The inevitable resentments here are terrible for building a culture of hospitality, and make hiring a challenge, a challenge that Meyer hopes to address through his new fee structure.

A guest dining in a restaurant has only a limited vision of what went into the success or failure of the service they experienced. Dishes coming out late, soup being served lukewarm, the restaurant being understaffed, and so forth, are inevitably going to be attributed by a customer, consciously or unconsciously, to the waitstaff, who probably aren't actually responsible. And the flip side—actions a waiter has taken, or not taken, that sabotage the customer experience, may be utterly invisible to the customer: failing to be a team player, for example. This is why one of Meyer's expressed goals with his new policy is to substitute the judgment of his management for the judgment of his customers in compensating particular employees.

Money changes everything.

On top of this, tipping is awkward. It rudely breaks the enchantment of the hospitality experience and makes it feel more mercenary than it needs to be. Having to calculate a gratuity brings customers crashing down to Earth with a requirement to do math and make ethical judgments at the end of what was otherwise (ideally) a seamless, even magical, experience.

But you're not Danny Meyer, so what should you do?

There is a lot to be said for making the moves that Danny Meyer is making to eliminate tipping, *if you're Danny Meyer*. The problem is that you're not Danny Meyer, who has an extraordinarily popular and packed stable of restaurants in the unique NYC dining scene.

For the rest of us, there are practical considerations. Here are a few to think about before making the leap:

- **Competition.** Will customers understand that you've not actually become more expensive, you just appear that way?

- **Slow periods.** The unfairness of a sub-minimum wage for tipped employees is of undeniable value to employers, especially at intermittently busy restaurants. If nobody comes in—it's raining, it's snowing, there's a game on— the wages aren't going to kill you.

- **_Tax implications._** Consult your accountant. They may not be pretty (the implications, that is; your accountant, I'm sure, is lovely).

- **_Will you lose that front of house flair?_** Danny Meyer is an acknowledged master of hospitality, and his establishments are known for their exceptionally well-selected, well-trained, well-managed front of house employees who bring a sense of both empathy and performance to what they do. Which makes Meyer in many ways the exception, even the outlier. If, by contrast, you're employing waitstaff whom you've selected without care, trained only minimally, and supervised not at all, you may need to continue to depend on your customers to keep them honest. Because nobody else is.

"AND YOUR POINT IS?"

Key Principles from Chapter 7:
Movie Making and Magic

▶ Your challenge is to envision what a state of "pleasure" or "enjoyment" looks like for your guest and work on putting together the individual pieces that will make up this whole. Think of this approach as "directing a movie with your customer as the star."

▶ Strive to *enchant* your guests, to bring them under a spell, to transport them from the tedium of a workaday life to a place that is in some sense magical.

▶ Consider the scenography approach used by The Ritz-Carlton Hotel Company that allows them to direct an emotionally powerful "movie" at each of their properties. To do so involves creating a property-wide theme and supporting it with design elements, lighting, cast participation, and more. But the single most important element in making a scenography approach succeed is creativity on the part of the GM and staff of the individual hotel in question.

▶ In addition to an overriding hotel theme, pay attention to the smaller touchpoints, individual *scenes*, if you will, each of which may require guest by guest adjustment.

▶ Experiences are the luxuries that customers are seeking today. Whether they're young and looking for adventure and excitement, or older and checking off a bucket list, more and more customers want to learn, to experience, to take part in something that they can look back on with pride.

▶ It's a dangerous mistake to think of the millennial generation as hard-edged technocrats. On the contrary, this young generation craves personal experiences.

▶ Change for change's sake is hazardous because the goal of customer service and the customer experience isn't buzz, it's loyalty. However, customers do desire change and excitement as well, which means getting the right balance of novelty and consistency is always going to be a tricky but necessary challenge.

8

The "Chocolate Tastes Better When It's Being Shared" Theorem

"Our customer set is so busy that these precious moments of travel are often their best chance to reconnect with each other. We strive to facilitate these connections."

—LISA HOLLADAY, VP for Global Brand Marketing, The Ritz-Carlton Hotel Company

"My goal in life is to make you a hero to your spouse."

—MARK HARMON, CEO, Auberge Resorts

One of the most powerful ways to serve guests and to become irreplaceable in their eyes is to facilitate relationships between your customers and the people your customers care about, on-site and off. Becoming a conduit for such relationships is the focus of this chapter, which is divided into two parts. Part I focuses on facilitating sharing between guests and their friends in the online and mobile world, and Part II discusses facilitating relationships between guests in the physical world.

Part I: Facilitating Online and Mobile Sharing

Remember the old step-by-step sequence of travel? First, plan your itinerary and save up enough money. Then, go on the trip and shoot a few rolls of film along the way. Only *then* would you involve your friends, or at least try. You'd develop that film into slides (slides!) and try to shanghai your neighbors and friends to come over and watch a carousel worth of your memories, a few of them inserted, inevitably, upside down or backward.

Travel today no longer follows this clear "before, during, and after" pattern. It's all "during," and the "during" is spent with your friends and loved ones, wherever in the world they may be. Friends are, in a sense, always along for the ride: kibitzing, advising, and being advised by you as they plan their own trips while you're taking yours. Boston Consulting Group has attempted to quantify this: "For a four-day leisure trip, the average consumer spends 42 hours online dreaming about, researching, planning, and making reservations, and then sharing their experiences while they travel or when they get back home."[31]

This kind of social sharing is the reality today in every arena of hospitality. In dining, customers share course by course photos of their meals ("foodographs") in real time. In live entertainment, fans attend concerts and switch perspectives throughout, between the unmediated live experience and viewing or streaming it on their video camera's tiny screen. Even in matters of health care, tweets and status updates from inside the ER are not unheard of, notably from professional athletes who've suffered serious game-time injuries. In addition, getting medical opinions from off-site friends and family members before and even during some procedures is far from rare.

This inclination to share is certainly not limited to any one generation, but it is especially pronounced among millennials, a sociable generation prone to expressing themselves online as well as in real life (IRL), particularly in the many arenas where online and offline activities and circles of friends overlap. Offline, they're more likely than other generations to shop, dine, and travel with groups, whether these are organized interest groups, less formal groupings of peers, or excursions with extended family, according to Boston Consulting Group data.[32] When online, millennial share their habits on Facebook, Snapchat, and other social networking sites, and the opinions they offer on Yelp, TripAdvisor, and Amazon, reflect their eagerness for connection. In addition, their online alerts to friends and followers that show off where they are, where they're coming from, and where they're headed reflect and affect behavior in the physical world.

Millennials don't consume food, beverages, services, products, or media in silence. They eat noisily (so to speak) and very visually. They review, blog, and Tumblr, update Wikipedia entries, and post You-Tube, Vine, and Instagram videos. Often these posts concern their consumption activities, interests, and aspirations. All told, as Boston Consulting Group reports, "the vast majority of millennials report taking action on behalf of brands and sharing brand preferences in their social groups."[33]

Again, this social sharing behavior encompasses every generation in the marketplace today. (Even the venerable Silent Generation—born in the mid-1920s to early 1940s—has long moved on from shooting slides and loading them into slide carousels.) Customers today of all ages shop, dine, and travel socially. Factors that support this behavior include the ubiquity of smart phones; customers' effortless ability to share their experiences and reviews on sites like Yelp and TripAdvisor; and the ease of organizing friends, families, and unaffiliated interest groups online in ways that result in real-life meet-ups, dinners, dates, drinks, and events.

Helping Your Guests Collect Social Currency

Why do customers decide to share? One factor that's worth pondering is the idea that customers share to elevate their status. A photo of a superb meal at a top restaurant is a source of pride as much as a memento, such as a souvenir menu, would be. Elevating status isn't necessarily about spending money somewhere fancy; it can be a well-planned excursion to an isolated yurt, pictures and videos of which are then proudly shared socially. Status these days looks different than it did in the old, more marketer-driven age of clearly graduated status increments, such as the climb from GM brand to GM brand—the long-established aspiration of trading in your Chevy for a Cadillac (-ack, -ack, -ack, to use the boomer phraseology of Billy Joel.)

One way purchases and experiences can increase status is by turning your customers into "discoverers" in the eyes of their friends, loved ones, and acquaintances. As a study by The Futures Company recently showed, customers are taking more and more pride in discovering things for themselves, including products and services for sale, and in being recognized by their peers for being "first." The medium of exchange, in other words, is social currency. As a hospitality professional, any effort and creativity you can invest in finding ways to help customers collect this social currency for use in building and maintaining their own relationships will simultaneously help your business.[34]

Lisa Holladay, VP for global brand marketing, The Ritz-Carlton Hotel Company:

> One of the things we find that our luxury travelers have in common is an interest in collecting experiences. So anything that our properties can do that's unique, whether it's right on property or something we turn our guests onto in the city that they wouldn't have thought of before or that isn't regularly available, is going to be appreciated. Collecting experiences creates kind of a personal history that is now there for you to share with your friends, your family members.
>
> The social aspect of sharing your discoveries is very strong today, especially the visual sharing concept. It's about sharing who you are and where you've been and what you've discovered—sharing what's going on in your life with other people and using that as a way to make and strengthen connections. In a phrase, "If I don't have a picture of it on my phone, it didn't happen" is the essence of the sentiment I've been hearing lately from customers, especially younger customers.

This means that if your business isn't building social sharing opportunities into the customer experience, it's missing out on chances to delight your customers. The Ritz-Carlton does this unobtrusively yet effectively with the "shareable experiences" feature on their app, which helps guests document and share memories. Guests can modify and enhance their travel photos with digital stamps, titles, and filters (specific to the particular property and its geographic location) to create retro travel posters to share via social media or to save as digital souvenirs. Guests can either post to their own social networks or in conjunction with the official #RCMemories "Let us stay with you" campaign on Twitter.

Sir Richard Branson, rather more brashly, encouraged social sharing at the grand opening of his Chicago Virgin Hotel by inviting guests at the opening to "Sleep with Richard—we promise we'll tell." Guests, one at a time, were encouraged to recline in a lascivious position in one of Virgin's custom designed guestroom beds, while Branson was digitally entwined with them to create a salacious photo for social distribution. And for perhaps the most integrated application of social hospitality, check out Hotel 1888 in Sydney, Australia. Better known as the "Instagram Hotel," it facilitates social sharing throughout its customer experience, with predetermined "selfie spaces" and an "Instagram walk" the hotel has mapped out for guests. By celebrating the role of the hotel and its environs as backdrop, 1888 makes sure it gets in the picture as well.

(These opportunities, by the way, don't only need to highlight your property, but can alternatively bring your guests together by helping them share any kind of travel-related recommendations. A good example of this is how Hilton Worldwide makes good use of its twitter handle, @HiltonSuggests, to encourage and share recommendations from one traveler to the next on what to do and see anywhere in the general vicinity of a Hilton property.)

DO YOUR BUNS LOOK GOOD ON INSTAGRAM?

Do your buns look good on Instagram? Chili's Restaurants has committed to making sure that theirs will. Chili's, the (sort of) Tex-Mex casual dining chain, is spending millions of dollars to make their food look more photogenic, more "shareable." For example, Chili's has started using an egg wash to give its hamburger buns a photogenic glaze that "glistens" (the adjective comes from Wyman Roberts, CEO of Chili's parent company, Brinker International); it's trying out a new way of stacking ribs to make them look better in photos; and it's switching to sexy stainless steel baskets that will fetchingly hold its fries.[35]

All this demonstrates a good understanding of the "if I don't have a photo of it on my phone, it never happened" aspect of the customer experience that so many of today's customers are looking for. It's important for them to experience the world visually and share it before, during, and after the purchasing decision.

Part II: Facilitating Relations Between Guests IRL (In Real Life)

One of the first times I talked with Mark Harmon, the hotelier responsible for Auberge Resorts' stable of small ultra-luxury hotels, I asked Harmon about his goals. Rather than replying with the kind of pat, conventional answer a CEO usually gives, he told me, with a mischievous smile, "My goal in life is to make you a hero to your spouse." By this Harmon means making the person who booked the reservation look good and making the couples who stay with him feel good in their time together. I find this such a telling goal and so central to Auberge Resorts' success. If Harmon were more conventional, more shortsighted, he might set his aims on a more traditional hospitality industry target: making his hotels the top small Five Star properties in their zip codes, for example. But Harmon focuses on his customers' goals rather than his own. As he puts it, "In the big scheme of things, how often as a couple do you really—I mean really—get away from the kids and get to connect in a stress-free setting? This is important, and we take it seriously. We're honored that guests let us be the setting for that connection, and we strive to make sure that the touches we add [help] make for a memorable time together here."

To build brand value in hospitality, it helps to take the approach Harmon does at his Auberge Resorts: to focus on facilitating the relationships that guests have with each other while enjoying your service and setting. Focusing on how your hospitality experience is shared by two or more guests, and to facilitate such sharing between them, requires you to accept that while your business may be the star, or at least a star, of *your* life, for your customers it represents something different. In hospitality, a brand often insinuates itself best into a customer's life, memory, and loyalty by being a backdrop to the story of their lives, as experienced with their friends and family.

Restaurants are one of the purest examples of this, providing, as they do, the settings for marriage proposals, love affairs, breakups, arguments, and, according to every mob drama that I've ever enjoyed, the occasional professional hit. Not to mention the more prosaic: business meetings, shared sunsets, and outings with coworkers. Once you zone in on this inherent reality of the restaurant setting, there are creative ways that this phenomenon can be supported and enhanced and, not incidentally, anchored in the customers' memories as being associated with the setting in question: your restaurant.

An elegant example of this is the Wine Library at the Selanne Steak Tavern in Laguna Beach, California. Here, guests can put their signature on a now-empty bottle of wine they've shared on a special occasion, and the Tavern's waitstaff will give it a place of honor on one of the Wine Library's book-style shelves. The Wine Library, says the tavern's Director of Operations, Leo Fenn III, "is about having and remembering great experiences.

Dining with close people/friends/family and enjoying delicious wines are what contribute to a great experience, and we want our guests to remember that previous, great experience" on return visits.

A service provider can fall into the trap of over-planning, over-theming, over-glitzing up the service environment and, consequently, take all the breathing room out of their customers' experience. It's an egotistical move, or at least comes off that way, by sending the message that customers should spend all their time and attention focusing not on the drama of their own lives but rather on the business's fabulousness. There are even restaurants with the hubris to instruct you on the proper manner in which to eat their food. This means, of course, that they are spending time *creating* food that requires such instructions. There are sommeliers who are so fascinated by their insider knowledge that they don't realize you're there for a somber occasion and you couldn't care less about the minutiae of wine, let alone the tale the sommelier's weaving of their most recent junket to Napa. And, of course, there's the overly chatty waiter who is continually interrupting and trying to one-up the guests, so enthralled with his own wonderfulness that he can't see that the couple at the table are trying to decide whether to adopt a child, overthrow a government, or run away together. This is unfortunate. To be successful, service businesses must give guests enough leeway to allow them to live out the drama and fantasy of their lives with the people who matter to them.

Mark Hoplamazian, Hyatt CEO:

We're trying to meet people where they are, understand what's going on with them, and help them to be their best. Whether that means staying with us while you're with your son, who's going through chemo, or you're there because you're celebrating an anniversary or because you've got a difficult discussion to have with your boss. What we think we can do is bring ourselves to those interactions, those human engagements, in a way that helps people be more effective, be at their best, be their happiest.

HOW "SHAREABILITY" MAKES THIS VENERABLE BRAND AN (UNLIKELY) HIT WITH TODAY'S DINERS

Being conducive to shared consumption has positioned certain unlikely brands for success with guests today. Case in point: the venerable, perennially unhip Melting Pot restaurant chain. Having dinner at any of The Melting Pot's 132 locations is an inescapably social experience. Diners share *everything* at the table: the cheesy (or chocolatey) fondue, the protein options that are spread on cutting boards around the table, the pots of boiling bouillon in which to cook those proteins. All within close proximity and with the rubbed shoulders inherent to the snug, comfy booth arrangement of the restaurants.

The Melting Pot will probably never (okay, *definitely* never) be a foodie destination or a hangout for locavores. Yet among its fans it's truly beloved. Fans who, in my very incomplete and informal survey, skew relatively young—especially surprising considering its significant price point. In the time I spent recently with CEO Bob Johnston of Front Burner Brands, the restaurant group that owns and manages The Melting Pot restaurants, our discussion frequently centered on tales of couples and families and affinity groups (teams, support groups, and such) who come back time after time because they've connected with the restaurant as being "their" place.

(This connection-via-gooey-goodness is historically apt. Although I doubt many diners at The Melting Pot are interested in this historical note, you may be: The original fondue craze itself coincided with and was fueled by the sexual revolution, according to food historian David Sax; the idea being that the insistently communal nature of the fondue setup would ensure a dinner party where you quickly became intimate with—and perhaps only a little later *very* intimate with—a small group of friends.[36] As Sax puts it, "There were no individual portions, no fondue for one—it was a meal of forced intimacy." Although that "key party" era has passed—as far as I know, although perhaps I'm just not getting invited!—the sharing aspect of The Melting Pot setup continues to be central to its success.)

This is an astute and effective way to serve today's customers. And while you may have been trained throughout your career to think your job is to entice customers into having a relationship directly with your business, in hospitality, when you want your customers to become loyal to your business, your best shot may lie in facilitating their relationships with others.

Catering to Family and Special Interest Groups

These relationships aren't always the couples that Harmon highlighted with his "making you a hero to your spouse" comment. There's another, growing marketplace reality to consider: Customers are, more often than ever, coming together in unusual groupings to consume travel, lodging, and food service. This means that if you're only making your business comfortable for customers who do business with you as couples or as a nuclear family, you're falling behind the times.

A lot of factors are feeding into this reconfiguration of the customer base. For one thing, young people are traveling more with their parents—they're doing *everything* more with their parents, actually. One of the most revolutionary facts about the millennial generation is that, to a surprising degree, they get along with their parents. Joeri Van den Bergh and Mattias Behrer, authors of *How Cool Brands Stay Hot,* an insightful book about marketing and the millennial generation, suggest that a very high percentage of this generation who are still teens even think of their parents as best friends; 85 percent of millennials who were teens at the time of their research named one of their parents as their best friend, rather than naming a peer. It's unclear how this sentiment carries over once these teens are in their twenties and thirties, but it's a striking finding. In addition, more than a third of this generation say they influence which products their parents buy, which shops and restaurants they visit, and which trips they take.

Another contributing factor is the increase in single-person households worldwide at all income levels, with a related increase of single travelers coming together in alternative groupings. Miguel Moital, a professor at Bournemouth University's School of Tourism: "I see more people traveling for an interest or hobby. People increasingly want to combine travel with their interest; they want to share, learn, and improve their skills; and they want to meet new people and see more of the world while they do so."[37]

The types of groups that travel together—or who come together after traveling individually from far-flung locations—vary widely: from marathon runners to hunters, from religious groups to salsa dancers. Not to mention the impossible to overlook Red Hat Society (or as The Simpsons memorably renamed them: "The Last of the Red Hat Mamas"). As with other novel groupings of travelers, these middle aged and older women would not, by and large, know each other in the course of their everyday lives, but have been able to organize their get-togethers fluidly and with ease thanks to internet-era communication.

And consider this: four out of five US households are not traditional (if that's really the right term) mom, dad, and pre-collegiate kids. Many are single parent, multigenerational, grandkids living with grandparents, roomies, parents with older "boomerang" kids—you name it. (In some demographics extended families are particularly pervasive: while one in six Americans overall live in a multigenerational setup, the percentage is significantly higher for Asian Americans—26 percent, African Americans—23 percent, and Hispanic Americans—22 percent.)[38]

Part of the way to meet this challenge is in the design and configuration of hospitality environments. Take the newly opened (and exhaustingly named) Four Seasons Resort Orlando at Walt Disney World Resort, which is the first non-Disney hotel on park property. This new Four Seasons undertaking, being purpose-built from scratch, provided an opportunity for Four Seasons, in collaboration with its development partner on the project, the Silverstein Group, to come up with solutions to the challenges involved. "Orlando is a market that many people visit along with extended multigenerational families," says Christopher Hunsberger, Four Seasons Hotels and Resorts' EVP of global products and innovation.

"We accommodate this with multiple room configurations. We can put two rooms together. We can put four rooms together. We can put a whole floor together. We can put a half a floor together. You can have a section of a hotel and have it feel very private and very secluded to you."

But multigenerational travel isn't necessarily about making it possible for your guests to be together every second of the day, says Hunsberger. "We know there are times when that multigenerational family wants to be together. There are times when they want to be able to separate from one another. So we have to respond to this; we have, for example, three very distinctly designed pool areas to accommodate multigenerational travel" during the times families want to be together, as well as the times they want to be apart. A family pool with a gradually sloping, beach-style entry is intended to be inviting to young swimmers, an adults-only pool offers a more spa-like atmosphere, and a "splash zone"-themed pool is exactly as you'd imagine it: the place to congregate and recreate when the oldsters are getting on the youngsters' nerves.

In a much more serious environment, Mayo Clinic, the world-renowned hospital and health care organization, provides "destination medicine"—the collaboration of experts from a range of specialties to provide diagnosis and treatment, or a treatment plan, for what are often very serious cases. Because coming to Rochester, Minnesota, (or to another of Mayo's locations) can be a family affair, and because the definition of family has been changing so quickly, Mayo builds out its exam rooms to accommodate large, fluid groups of families and friends, including commissioning specially shaped sofas that work as seating for one or two visitors or for half a dozen, if needed, depending on the number of loved ones visiting.[39]

Room and facility re-configuration are only a small part of what it takes to embrace intergenerational hospitality. It's about using your creativity and your resources as a hospitality organization to facilitate the connections between generations of guests.

Here's what Ritz-Carlton's Lisa Holladay, VP for global brand marketing, has to say:

The trend toward more and more intergenerational travel is impacting our hotels, not just from a design standpoint but from a programming standpoint as well. It's one reason we launched the new, expanded "Ritz Kids" programming last year, because we saw families moving away from the idea of "I'm going to leave the kids at home," or "Let's leave them with grandma and grandpa," or "Let's leave them with the nanny," to an approach of "I want to connect with my kids; I want to spend time with my kids."

Our customer set is so busy that these precious moments of travel are often their best chance to reconnect with each other. We strive to facilitate these connections between our guests. Ritz Kids provides our guests globally with immersive programming that educates, entertains, and hopefully inspires our youngest guests, including content created by Jean-Michel Cousteau's Ocean Futures Society, exclusively for The Ritz-Carlton. The results? Guests with children are three times more likely to say their stay was enhanced if their children received special treatment.

In designing their program with Cousteau, Ritz-Carlton leadership felt it was important that everything possible be localized in thrust and content. "We've designed it with Cousteau so that an individual property can bring forward programming that is unique and interesting for that location," says Holladay, "rather than just a canned set of curricula that you pull off the shelf."

The opportunities to help the generations connect are at least as strong in food service as they are in lodging. Casual restaurant Ruby Tuesday was a special place in my relationship with my kids when they were younger, and there must be other families with a similar feeling about the chain, because Ruby Tuesday embraces this even to the point of custom printing gift cards with your kid's picture on it. And Chick-fil-A's "Daddy-Daughter Date Night" is a very special tradition for a certain group of fathers and daughters.

Regardless of the occasion, if you take your role of facilitation and support seriously, if you provide a stage, a backdrop for the relationships of your customer, you can become, and remain, their provider of choice.

Lattes and Laptops: Supporting "Alone Together" Time

Beyond the ties of families, the sparks of lovers, and the affinities of affinity groups, one type of relationship that you can benefit from facilitating probably doesn't even qualify as a true relationship. It's being *around* people, rather than being *with* them. This is the desire of many guests for "alone together" time.

Including—at this very moment—me. I often find myself writing my chapters and articles from my "field office": a booth at the charming, funky Madison Diner a couple of blocks from my home. On its face, this makes little sense. I have other places to work, yet I choose to work here, and have done so for years in a variety of diners and similar noisy (but not *too* noisy) public spaces. And I'm not the only one doing private work in public. Today's customers are doing a lot of the same. The Futures Company dubbed such customers, who paradoxically crave a communal setting in which to do private work, "Latte and Laptop" customers.

As designer David Rockwell puts it, today's customers "want . . . different options to work and socialize," and "don't want what they do to be predetermined by [inflexible] architecture," preferring "flexible public spaces and open layouts." All of which makes psychological sense.

In fact, just recently, researchers at Yale, using chocolate as their study material (I bet a bit of *that* disappeared from storeroom shelves from time to time), concluded that chocolate tastes best when two or more people are eating it together. When the study's participants (an easy position to fill, I'm guessing) tasted chocolate together, they judged it as tasting better than when they ate it alone. This held true even if the two people eating the chocolate didn't share a single word with each other. As the study's authors summarize, "Sharing an experience with another person, [even] without communicating, amplifies one's experience."[40]

The New Business Center

Two decades ago it may have felt kind of cool as a traveler to cocoon yourself in the business center at a hotel, an isolation tank so well-stocked with paper clips, scotch tape, and a hole punch—everything you needed for business in that era. But now that business and leisure have become almost inseparable (due to the smartphone, tablet, and laptop), the isolated business center is feeling obsolete. The Ritz-Carlton Istanbul, in fact, completely shut theirs down until they could come up with a better alternative, which they ultimately did, replacing the old business center with a new and unusual "living room" concept. In The Ritz-Carlton Istanbul's Living Room, there's little to clue you in that this even is a business center, other than the fact that a few of the bar-style tables are augmented by Macs with twenty-inch flat screens. The environment looks more like a pool hall and speakeasy, one that's complete with a fully stocked bar (and, when needed, a bartender), overstuffed chairs, professional grade pool table, and a wall-to-wall view of the Bosphorus river. Ritz-Carlton Istanbul's GM Max Zanardi:

> *A few years ago—before computer technology and the cloud changed everything—if you were running a hotel business center, customers would grade you on whether you had staples in the stapler, and supplies in the drawer like the paper and envelopes that they might need. And as long as it was fully stocked, people were grudgingly content using a basic business center in a hotel when they needed it.*
>
> *But look at an average hotel business center today. I think it has the highest concentration of misery in the entire city! Today, it's totally uncool to be in a business center. Nobody wants to be there; it's the worst, loneliest place of every hotel. We replaced it here with what we call a living room, right here on the lobby level, with one of the best views in the city.*
>
> *Our thinking was, if you were at home and deciding where to put a stationary computer, where would you put it? You'd put it*

in a nice, central but quiet room where you can see outside. Maybe
you would have a beer with your email, or here you can have a cus-
tom-made martini prepared by your own bartender.

Me, I've never gotten good results by combining martinis with writing, but when I was in Istanbul, Zanardi's innovation did allow me to intersperse my work on the computer with several leisurely games of pool with my ten-year-old, bathed in the light that was afforded by the wall-to-wall view of the river and city. Which certainly felt better than trudging down an obscure hallway to the dreaded "center of business misery" that used to be a hallmark of a modern hotel.

"AND YOUR POINT IS?"

Key Points for Chapter 8:
"The Chocolate Tastes Better When
It's Being Shared" Theorem

▶ Strive to facilitate relationships between your customers and the people your customers care about, on-site and off. Being a conduit for such relationships can be roughly divided into two parts:

  ✦ facilitating sharing between guests and their friends in the online and mobile world

  ✦ facilitating relationships between guests in the physical world

▶ Guests today are sharing constantly. They share as they decide to travel, while they're preparing to travel, while they're traveling, and as soon as they're done traveling. The same is true in food and beverage ("foodographs" taken before a single bite of food is consumed) and in practically every other arena of commerce today.

▶ If you aren't building opportunities for social sharing into the customer experience, you're missing out on opportunities to delight and retain your customers. The medium of exchange today is "social currency," so invest effort and creativity in helping customers collect this social currency to share with their friends.

▶ While your business may be the star of *your* life, for your customers it represents something different. In hospitality, a brand often insinuates itself best into a customer's life, memory, and loyalty by being a backdrop to the story of their lives, as experienced with their friends and family.

▶ Today, intergenerational consumption of hospitality is important. Extended families, and adult children traveling with their parents, are very important demographics in both lodging and foodservice. Whatever you can do to accommodate these types of groupings will be appreciated and will help grow and sustain your business.

▶ Many guests today desire "alone together" time, a communal setting where, paradoxically, they can do private work.

9

How the Digital Revolution Has Changed Your Customers

The only sense that is common, in the long run,
is the sense of change.[41]—E. B. White

Today's customers think differently about customer service and the customer experience, and this is true both inside and outside of hospitality. Consumers today are buying (or deciding not to buy), raving about your customer service (or telling their friends to avoid you), enhancing (or depressing) your bottom line based on factors your business may have never considered.

It's important to get a fix on this, and quickly, because the changes that customers have already begun to clamor for are just a whisper compared to what's about to come. Every trend that affects your business subtly today will actively confront your company within a few years, as younger customers enter the marketplace and revolt against the archaic ways that you're still doing business.

The Arrival of the Millennial Generation

A key reason for the urgency of this message is demographic. Millennial customers, born between 1980 and 2000 (give or take), are the largest generation in United States and world history—even larger than the baby boom at its height, and significantly larger than the generation just before them, Generation X. Millennials will soon be bringing to your property or dining room the greatest spending power of any generation to date.

Millennials are the first more or less completely "digitally native" generation. Their expectations as customers have been shaped by a lifetime of immersion in the fast-evolving worlds of online commerce, search engines, and on-the-go connectivity. These young people have always been exposed to cell phones, email, and the web. They've rarely waited in line at the bank or awaited the arrival of a letter by mail; GPS has kept them from ever needing to ask for directions or read a map; they've seldom had their musical choices limited to the radio or what can fit on a mass-marketed CD.

Customers in Every Generation are "Turning Millennial"

Millennials are important because of their sheer numbers and direct economic importance *and* because their preferences and behaviors are increasingly bleeding into the customer behavior of older generations. So it makes good economic sense to focus on millennial guest expectations both because their own purchasing power is valuable (and rapidly growing) and because their digitally driven expectations are spreading so quickly to other generations. The standard expectation of a seventeen-year-old or twenty-five-year-old guest today will be mirrored in the expectations of her mom and dad as well in a very, very short time.

Regardless of our age bracket, are well on our way to "becoming millennials" in terms of our service expectations. As Christopher Hunsberger of Four Seasons Hotels and Resorts puts it, "millennials are an important group of guests in their own right. But their significance is more than that. They're a unique group in terms of their impact on the rest of our customer base. The behaviors and expectations of the millennial group tend to shape the thinking of the rest of us."

Serving guests today and tomorrow means finding the best ways to streamline the hospitality experience via technology, and it means delivering the warmest, most genuine human-to-human hospitality where such human interaction makes a difference. This isn't easy. Adapting your mindset to successfully serving new and rapidly evolving customers will take your attention, creativity, and hard work.

What Digital Has Done to Your Guests

Here's what the digital revolution has done to your guests. It might not be pretty, but it is (as annoying people annoyingly say) what it is. Customers now expect every business, in every industry, to achieve "digital parity," (a term I picked up from Jay Coldren at Marriott), meaning to be as easy to do business with as what customers have encountered in the very best online and self-service solutions.

- *Interactions should be intuitive, efficient, and fast, and shouldn't require unwanted, extraneous human intervention by either the customer or your employees.* In a hospitality context, this means that guests expect a streamlined, seamless, technology supported experience. Shelley Meszoly, regional director of sales and marketing at Fairmont Southampton (Bermuda): "Your service needs to be easy to book, it needs to be easy to buy, it needs to be available through all their desired channels: on their phone, their iPad, or in person, with no glitches and no holdups. [Guests] expect everything they need to be in front of them, effortlessly available, entirely transparent, and ready to be used."

- *Customers should have control over their own account details, including the ability to modify their service preferences, and the service provider should have omni-channel access to this information as well.* In a hospitality context, this means, among other things, that guests expect service providers to have access to the guest's entire customer history and guest preferences, without the guest needing to repeat or rekey any of it. This information should be (discreetly) available, with zero notice and no lag time, across properties and everywhere within a property, whether a guest is interacting with the employee in person, on the phone, over the Internet, or via mobile.[42] It also means that guests are starting to expect functionality along the lines of the Hilton Hotels app's functionality that allows you to choose your own specific room, literally down to the room number (although, as of press time, without useful indicators such as "which rooms have connecting doors"), from available choices, or of the new Four Seasons app's ability to summon housekeeping from offsite—when a guest realizes they left their privacy light on back at the property but still want their room cleaned before they get back.

- *Service should move quickly, and time restrictions should be malleable, like they are online.* In a hospitality context, this means guests expect speedy service and flexible hours, just like they're used to online. (Think about it: when you're shopping online, you never have to wait in line to check out and pay. And online, a site is always open to serve you on your own schedule, with no waiting and no "sorry, we're closed.") For example, guests are starting to expect to be able to order during the interval *between* the lunch and dinner hours—and to be able to order an item from the lunch menu during the dinner hour, and vice versa. It means that for room service to be relevant, it needs to get faster, perhaps *twice* as fast, á la Four Seasons' recently rolled out fifteen-minute room service promise. It means, in the foodservice context, that the variety of innovative tabletop tech solutions that allow guests to pay their bills without flagging a waiter or waiting for that waiter to run to the POS (point of sale device) to charge a guest's card are steps in the right direction, assuming that they're implemented with sensitivity.

This is a tough, hard-nosed set of expectations that guests are beginning to bring to your doorstep, and the industry needs to adapt to them, and soon.

Checking Out the Check-In Situation

Let's look at check-in, which offers in microcosm the issues that need to be resolved as we move into the future as an industry. Hoteliers have traditionally conceived of check-in as an important moment for high-touch service, rather than as a merely transactional function. They put great stock in finding ways to ensure that the check-in experience is personal and memorable. I, too, am in favor of these hospitable goals; the trouble comes when these goals are pursued at the expense of speed and efficiency, and without giving guests any choice in the matter. Modern hotel guests will inevitably compare the slow, benevolently authoritarian hotel check-in process with what they recently experienced via online booking and air travel, the systems that have allowed them to choose their exact preferred schedule and seat, make meal and special needs requests, and print out a boarding pass, all from the comfort of home.

This is the process, in fact, that has conveyed them to the front desk of the hotel, where they're now waiting grudgingly in line. And they'll likely find the contrast a bit absurd.

Stand in line. Wait for a front desk agent. Orally deliver intricate, intimate information to the agent. Watch him slowly and approximately enter this data on a DOS era computer terminal—the same data that an average consumer has used for online service transactions six times that same day. Allow the clerk to choose a room, based on only nominal knowledge of the guest's preferences. Wait to be handed a room key, at which juncture the clerk, in a suddenly resonant voice, asks that indiscreet question: "How many keys would you like, Ms.____ [last-name-I'm-going-to-say-particularly-loud-in-case-somebody-in-the-lobby-wants-to-know-if-you're-expecting-a-visitor]?" Finally, listen to the agent's canned recitation of the hotel's unique features. All before being finally liberated to go about your business.

Hotels would do well to find a way to resolve the check-in conundrum—and some of them are. Hilton, Marriott, Starwood, and Fairmont have recently implemented smartphone based check-in solutions. CitizenM, a stylish limited-service hotel chain in Europe, has entirely eliminated the front desk, replacing it with a bank of self-service check-in kiosks similar to those found in airports. Unlike your average airport, however, CitizenM has a cadre of truly engaging employees working the lobby: "Hi, and welcome. Have you been to CitizenM before? First time? Great, let me help you check in."

Although the employee offers to handle the check-in himself, he also indicates to the guest that the self-service approach is really a snap. True to his word, the kiosk technology is great. Typing in the first few characters of the guest's last name brings up the reservation details. Payment is confirmed with a swipe of the card, and instructions on the screen direct the guest to a box of blank key cards on the counter in front of the kiosk. Tapping on the screen encodes the keycard and a separate receipt pops out with the room number printed on it. All the while, the smartly dressed and eager staff members are nearby and available to help. Fast, efficient, and friendly.

HOW'S THAT
SMARTPHONE-AS-ROOM-KEY COMING?

Hilton made a bit of a splash some time back with its announcement that guest smartphones would soon function as room keys, and promising an aggressive schedule for the rollout. As it has turned out, this smartphone-as-room-key rollout has been slow going, both at Hilton and at its competitors. While some Hilton (and some Starwood, Marriott, and independent properties) have indeed launched the technology, simple economics are for the time being holding back a more widespread implementation.

The cost *per door* to retrofit a hotel with the smartphone-as-room-key is three hundred to five hundred dollars, a hard sell to make to a property owner, who for a 200-room hotel would have to go out and spend $60,000 to $100,000. On the other hand, any hotel property that's already fitted with "wave keycard to open" NFC functionality—or the "wave your wristband" approach of Great Wolf Lodge—can be refitted less expensively to being smartphone-enabled.

Not for Everyone

But the CitizenM model isn't to everyone's taste, nor is it right for every service environment. Says luxury hotelier Mark Harmon, chairman of Auberge Resorts: "I think the kiosk can come off as offensive, especially when you're paying a few more bucks for your room," as Harmon coyly understates it; a night at an Auberge property can easily reach the four digits. "I certainly share the goal of off-loading transactional details, just not forcibly off-loading them onto the guest."

Harmon prefers to "use a roving iPad to check people in without ever making them wait in line—and [hoteliers should] reconsider if they even need to make guests go through check-in at all. At Auberge, we often know our guests and their expected arrival ahead of time, and can welcome them and hand them their keys directly," without either cattle-call queuing or making guests perform the check-in work themselves.

When guests arrive at the David Rockwell-designed Nobu Hotel in Las Vegas, they're greeted by a concierge who takes them to their room via a dedicated elevator for a private in-room iPad registration. And at the Andaz in Maui, another design from David Rockwell replaces the standard single check-in desk. Rockwell describes it: "Cozy groupings of furniture provide a more welcoming and personal experience: Each individual check-in desk features different, unique touches, such as telescopes or sandpits." (I have to wonder how they ever got buy-in from housekeeping for *intentionally* bringing sand into the lobby for guests to track through the hotel!)

Whatever streamlining solution is applied to the check-in experience, once it is instituted, the job duties of the lobby staff can be redefined. While one staffer handles check-in, another can show guests around the lobby and explain the offerings and hours of the hotel's café and bar. A third can draw a map to a nearby museum or help guests hail a cab. The staff can focus, in other words, on making the guest experience better and more meaningful, instead of on queue control and laborious data entry.

Where Do Humans Fit in the Service Equation?

Building the right experience for today's customers requires you to think hard about an uncomfortable subject: where human employees are helpful to customers, and where they just get in the way.

Today's customers often *do* want you out of the way. Younger customers, in particular, hold different ideas about where human-powered service fits into the customer experience. Through years of experience with online and self-service solutions, they've grown used to the way technology can reduce the need for human gatekeepers to ensure accuracy and manage data. So the last thing they want is for your employees to gum up the works without adding value.

Think for a moment about how many transactions customers today routinely conduct without any human interaction. They make dinner reservations, sign up for classes, review schoolwork and grades, schedule and reschedule medical appointments. Previously, all these transactions required contact with another human. Now, thanks to technological advances, they can often be carried out without uttering a word to a single employee. In handling such transactions without the intervention of employees, customers have discovered that technology often takes care of such logistical functions faster and more capably than when employees insert themselves into the equation.

Meet the Jetsons

One of my secrets for creating a superior experience for today's customers is my (unauthorized) Jetsons' Approach to Customer Service, based on the 1962 television series set a hundred years in the future. It's a colorful little test you can use to determine the service functions that belong on either side of the human/technology divide—that is, which services you should off-load to technology and which ones you should keep in the hands of your employees.

Here's what customer service looks like in the Jetsons' vision of the future:

- *Much of the customer service is provided by machines.* And much of this machine-based service is actually self-service: ordering breakfast from an automated menu at home, recording telephone messages on rewriteable LP records. (They got this prediction at least 75 percent right.) And, of course, housecleaning via Rosie the Robot, the animatronic housekeeper with a New Yawk accent and an attitude to match. (Hilton Hotels is currently testing its answer to Rosie: a robot assistant cutely named for the brand's founder, Conrad Hilton. Powered by IBM Watson artificial intelligence, Connie is currently in residence at the Hilton McLean, Virginia, right in the heart of the D.C. sprawlosphere. And in a West Coast nod to Rosie, Aloft Cupertino Hotel in the heart of Silicon Valley recently deployed a personable little robot dubbed Botlr that can come to your floor—summoning the elevator for itself—to assist you with little items you need and such.)

- *The service provided by humans adds what people want out of human interaction: warmth and a little drama.* Consider the friendly southern accented receptionist who provides a warm greeting at the factory where George Jetson works, or consider Henry, the apartment building's superintendent who does a bit of handiwork here and there but whose primary function is to be buddies with the Jetson family.

This is a pretty solid model for dividing your operations. If a person can do the job better—meaning more flexibly, accurately, creatively, dramatically, or simply more pleasantly—assign that task to the warm-blooded. Otherwise, if the task/touchpoint is something that automation or computers with algorithms can handle better, be sure to offer self-service, "my account," or app-based functionality as at least an option for your customers.

The exceptions are when warmth comes at the expense of efficiency, or vice versa. Then, it's a judgment call. And there will be *many* judgment calls; don't get me wrong. Just one fascinating example of this, where human inefficiency has been found to be preferable, is Air New Zealand's business class plane interiors that are *intentionally* designed to require human intervention (turndown) at bedtime from a skilled flight attendant. While other business class carriers have seats designed to change fully automatically to and from a sleeping position, Air New Zealand decided this was a mistake because the turndown part of their service, while technically not necessary, was crucial to the passenger experience.

The futuristic Jetsonian approach, however, can be a magnet for mischief. Once you've saved resources by automating tasks and services, it's tempting to pocket the savings and call it a day. But improving automated customer service is no excuse to offer lousy human-powered service. Instead, take the resources recouped through digitization and focus them on meaningful human interactions in the places where they count.

WHERE TABLET-BASED ORDERING AND HUMAN WARMTH COEXIST

If you bring tablet-based ordering to your restaurant, be sure you think out what you're doing, and be especially sure your waitstaff doesn't use it, consciously or unconsciously, as an excuse to offer slacker "why don't you look at the tablet already?" service. Believe me, this is a very big danger. A renowned chain of steakhouses in the Midwest—that will remain nameless—has switched recently to an iPad-based menu, and the answer to any question you might ask a server is responded to exactly thus: "you can read all about it on the tablet."

By contrast, if you're looking for a restaurant to benchmark that has a well-thought-out, Jetsonian hybrid approach—human warmth *and* automated service—consider looking at Colorado Springs' Natural Epicurean, located on the campus of the Broadmoor. Particularly popular with young families, as well as singles and couples in their late teens and twenties, Natural Epicurean is a restaurant devoted to natural foods that fit a variety of diets and food restrictions. In pursuit of this goal, The Natural Epicurean offers its guests the option of using a tablet-based menu to assist them with their dining choices. The tablet menu allows guests to:

- Select a meal based on food restrictions or dietary requirements (for example, select "desserts under four hundred calories" and you see what is available)

- Browse every menu on the item to see very specific information (calorie count, sodium content, etc.) about any items that are catching your eye

- Allow you to consider substitutions for item ingredients and to see the resulting difference in nutritional value

But here's the difference at The Natural Epicurean: Not only is the technology spiffy, but the waitstaff clearly doesn't consider it a replacement for the service—the warmth, recognition, and flexibility—that they as humans are so well qualified to provide.

At no point did I feel pressure from my waitress to figure everything out for myself electronically. The tablet was merely an adjunct, to save a customer with dietary restrictions from having to awkwardly ask question after question while nailing down choices (and perhaps to prevent the ridiculous ad libs waiters sometimes are forced to make when asked complex nutritional and ingredient-related questions on the fly).

The waitress was there for when questions came up that the tablet could not have been prepared to answer, such as my eleven-year-old son asking for help finding "the least healthy item on the menu." While she didn't oblige with a direct answer, she did clarify that the "ancient grains" bun on the bison burger could be swapped out for a white one, and the pesto on the burger replaced with American cheese (excuse me a moment while I hang my head in parental shame).

A large study of the hospitality industry recently by J. D. Power confirmed the importance of retaining human-delivered service touches, even as automation comes to the fore. Specifically, Power found that the *number* of employees with whom guests interact affects their overall satisfaction. Customers who interact more often with service staff, and with a broader cross-section of that staff, reported greater satisfaction. (The highest satisfaction was reported by guests who were served by four or more types of employees and the lowest by those who received no further service beyond front desk check-in.) "As hoteliers experiment with automated methods of check-in and check-out that tend to reduce the number of human touchpoints, it is important that they use the additional staff time gained to offer a warmer, more personalized experience for their guests," says Ramez Faza, senior manager of the global travel and hospitality practice at J. D. Power. "Hotels should never underestimate the power of the human element. Whether it's assisting a guest with a special request or a friendly greeting from staff members in the hallway, the people aspect plays a key role in guest satisfaction and loyalty."[43]

So, the name of the game is to take any savings you realize from automating transactional details and invest them in the live performance aspect of your business. I fear, though, that this is a game that few are going to play. Instead, as the airlines have done before them, shortsighted hospitality operators will pass the automation-driven savings along to their shareholders and consider themselves done. The problem with this approach is that it removes your differentiation, which is a recipe, ultimately, to put yourself out of business. Because if all you can offer is streamlining, what's left to distinguish the service experience in the minds and memories of your customers?

"Only great customer service allows you the 'price elasticity' that supports your bottom line so you can survive in this business," cautions Tom Colicchio. "I appreciate the pressure to reduce employees through technology, especially with the minimum wage going up, but if technology is deployed for that reason alone, it's a recipe for failure. Success in this business is not about that, it's about creating such a great offering that you can actually have some elasticity in pricing, because you are providing such a good experience. If you're cutting corners or substituting technology just to save money, it cuts out your competitive edge; your offerings will become the same as everyone else and your pricing will have to be as well. The only way you can move out of this trap, the value add that's going to get you there, is service and hospitality."

Full-Service Hotels: A Particular Kind of Magic Trick

A hotel, especially a full-service hotel, is a particular kind of a magic trick. It's the transformation of what by rights should be a commodity—chairs, table, a bed, a toilet that flushes properly—into something else: a place where lodgers become guests, where relationships are refreshed, where memories are created.

Superior hotels have long accomplished this with service personally delivered by exquisitely trained humans who remember guest names, who are alert to mood changes in guests, who strive to serve not only what a guest directly asks for, but what the guest may not even know that they're looking for.

The Luxury-Mobile Paradox

Fitting mobile, automated, and self-service offerings into this human-driven hospitality scenario is touchy. There's more, it would seem, that can go wrong than can go right, a reality that has deterred full-service—especially luxury—lodging brands from rushing in. While some Five Star hotels have made at least the partial leap (ultra-luxury Auberge Resorts has been offering iPad-based room service ordering for some time, as has Aria, the 4,004-room luxury behemoth in Las Vegas), the dominant sentiment has been "watch and wait."

But that's changing, with Ritz-Carlton hotels being the first out of the gate in mobilizing, so to speak, the luxury experience for its guests. (Not long afterward, The Ritz-Carlton's estimable competitor, Four Seasons Hotels and Resorts, rolled out its own intriguing app experience.) The Ritz-Carlton mobile experience includes poolside ordering, mobile room service, app-based service requests (replacing that toothbrush you accidentally discarded, the extra washcloth, soaps, or shoeshine touch-up you need before dinner), real-time device-agnostic folio review, mobile check-in, mobile check-out, and the nifty "shareable experiences" feature that I covered in chapter 8.

Mobile Check-in

Mobile check-in at The Ritz-Carlton starts with providing the guest with a personalized one-click link the day before arrival. Enter your anticipated arrival time and phone number, and at the appropriate time you'll get an SMS message to confirm that your room is ready, at which point you go to "mobile check-in" to pick up your keys. No further registration or identification is needed, unless required by law, and no additional credit card swipe.

The thing is, this being The Ritz-Carlton, the current front desk scenario, without all this new mobile check-in functionality, is hardly a hardship. The odds of having to wait in line for a surly, distracted, gum-chewing front desk clerk at The Ritz-Carlton or one of its estimable competitors is less likely than a direct lightning strike penetrating an underground bunker.

So what *does* mobile check-in buy you as a luxury hotel guest? It offers various functionality that travelers (including, The Ritz-Carlton tells me, the luxury travelers with whom they've spent two years researching and planning this app) appreciate. It allows these guests to handle their transactional details themselves, on a self-service basis, checking that everything is just as they want it (no more "is the card I have on file the one you want to use?" kind of gentle runaround, no more mistyping of hard to spell guest names, no more inability to double-check reservation details on your own). Thus giving the guest a more comfortable feeling of being both in the moment and in control.

Poolside Ordering

Now, picture this. You're poolside at The Ritz-Carlton. You can't track down one of their Ladies or Gentlemen, so you have to trudge all the way (twenty yards) to the pool bar, order your drink, and tote that tonic and gin all the way back to your poolside chair or cabana.

Tough, isn't it? It's also unlikely. The reality is, this "my kingdom for a waiter's attention" scenario is an unlikely one at a Ritz-Carlton or one of its worthy competitors. Rather, as I've discussed earlier, their employees are meticulously trained to recognize the most subtle eye contact or nod of a head, and come over to assist you before you need to ask for a thing or move a muscle.

So what, exactly, in this scenario would make a guest think they need the assistance of an app? It's more a question of guest preference than need. Sometimes, guests prefer to have a self-service experience, an experience that conforms to what they've gotten used to in the rest of their device-driven life. Not necessarily all of the time, but during those times when they don't want to interact (or interact before they're ready) with a human employee, when they want to browse available options within the privacy of their own skull, when they want a feeling of direct, self-service, DIY control.

The Future Is Now: How Ivy Uses IBM's Watson to Provide Artificial Intelligence-Driven Hospitality

There are some hotels that are already embracing the Jetsonian future, assigning less mission-critical tasks to automation while retaining the most sensitive tasks for handling by human employees.

One comprehensive approach to offering an on-site alternative to human intervention is Ivy, an artificial intelligence-driven system capable of handling, in real time, some 90 percent (according to its parent company, Go Moment) of the requests that come in from guests on property, without requiring a lick of human intervention.

Ivy is powered by IBM's Watson, the world-famous, Jeopardy-winning artificial intelligence (AI, also referred to as Cognitive) engine. Ivy uses this Watson engine to decipher and fulfill a wide variety of requests from hotel guests in real time.

Ivy is the brainchild of Raj Singh, President and CEO of its parent company, Go Moment. Singh is both a technologist and a kid-emeritus who grew up working hands-on in his family's hotels. Coming from this hospitality background, Singh tells me, made him aware of the detailed knowledge that would be required to ever automate the challenges that come up in hospitality, and the nuanced approach that would be required to do so in a manner that would draw guests closer to a hospitality brand rather than putting them off with a stilted, tone-deaf set of responses.

To pull this off, Singh knew he would need some powerful help. So when he heard that IBM had allocated $100 million for venture investments to support startups and businesses committed to leading a specific industry with cognitive applications powered by Watson, he jumped at the opportunity.

The resulting Watson-Ivy collaboration plays out as follows, starting at check-in, where the hotel's (human) front desk attendant asks the guest if they'd be willing to opt in to the Ivy system. If you opt in, says Singh, "you get a little welcome message when you get to your room that says, 'Micah, welcome to the W Los Angeles. How do you like your room so far?' You can reply, 'five stars, I love the view. Can I get a bottle of red wine? And I could use a few more hand towels.' Each request will be interpreted and dispatched to the correct department automatically using Watson categorization."

You can also—and these colorful examples are obviously mine, not Singh's—text "Wassup, People?! I asked for a king and got to my room and there's two queen beds instead" or "If I had a burning desire to have my ear as close as possible to the ice machine, I would have indicated that when I checked in. Now can I please have a quieter room?" and Ivy will reply "I'm very sorry to hear that; a bellman will soon be at your door to take you to the correct room." (Note: If you say "I freaking hate this place; beam me out of here," or otherwise express any kind of upset, Ivy bows out and a human is immediately dispatched, as I'll discuss below.)

Ivy is frequently called on to deliver instant answers to knowledge-based questions. For example, if a guest texts 'what is the WiFi password?,' it will deliver an answer instantly, with no humans needing to be involved. And when the "reply" needed is a task rather than information, that's in Ivy's skill set as well. In the example of asking for extra hand towels, Watson is able to route that request directly to the laundry for faster and better results. "That's what the Ivy platform does: It streamlines operations and automates most decisions that previously required distracting the front desk from the guest waiting to check in." This way, says Singh, "the guest is always the center of attention and always has all of the hotel's resources at their disposal. Now your request goes directly to the right department in a fraction of the time it would take the front desk to manually receive, log, and relay your request."

(Watson, you may remember, is essentially a "question-answering engine," initially developed by IBM to be able to decode the many ways a question can be asked on Jeopardy in essentially zero time—and get to that buzzer first! The answers, in other words, are not really the trick to Watson; any encyclopedia can do that part of the trick. It's the *questions* that matter. So while it might not seem like all of Watson's smarts are required to answer something like "What's the Wifi passcode?" the power of Watson is really coming in to play here to decode the many, many ways that a guest might make such a request. Fifteen different people might ask for the same thing in fifteen different ways: "What's the wireless passcode?" "How do I get on the internet? And so forth. Watson's involvement here is in detecting the intention behind the words. This keeps things effortless for the guest with Watson allowing the Ivy text responses to adapt to the guest, rather than the other way around.

Creating Ivy has required its creators to get down and dirty with the particular issues that come up at each particular client hotel. In doing so, they've found that there are about 1,400 issues that can come up, barring an outlier event such as a fire. According to Singh, more than half of these don't require human judgment on the other side, and that half account for a significant majority of the interactions that come up.

Of course, the issues that *don't* make up this "significant majority not requiring human judgment" should be of great concern to anyone considering deploying such a system. Because here's the rub: If an organization blows it on the items that do require true service recovery, it just doesn't matter how many mundane issues were correctly handled; that latter, emotionally-charged failure is what customers are going to remember.

So a concern I had when exploring Ivy—and that you should have before laying down your money for such a system—was whether Ivy's ability to answer the somewhat mundane majority of what comes up would cause its developers to develop hubris and inappropriately deploy Ivy to try to act as if she/he were human, with potentially guest-alienating results. So I wanted to find out how, and whether, "she" knows to escalate the texts received that require or would benefit from a human response.

Here, I've been so far reassured by the logic behind Ivy. Ivy is programmed to escalate any expressions of dissatisfaction to humans. According to Singh, "The first question that Ivy always asks the guest is 'How's everything going?' If any negative words are detected in that response or if the person says, one star, my sheets are dirty, my toilet's overflowing, and all those kind of common issues—we've got hundreds of them cataloged for every single hotel that is on our portfolio—we escalate any negative experiences from the customer instantly to the front desk and then track how quickly the desk agent follows up with them. So let's say you express that you're having a bad experience. Let's say you type 'my sheets are dirty.' Ivy knows what all of us in the hospitality business know: that 'dirty' is a really bad word. So we send that off to the front desk for personal attention. From the time the staff gets a text message and email alert, they usually have twenty minutes to resolve the issue before Ivy escalates the issue to the general manager."

(Ivy will also dispatch a human when Watson isn't entirely confident that it understands the meaning of a question or how to resolve it; for example, if a guest says something like "my internet is broken." From this, Ivy can detect that the guest is talking about the Internet, but doesn't have a way of resolving this issue of the Internet being broken, because

Watson may not be able to understand what 'broken' means in that context. In such a case, Singh says, "Ivy turns to an algorithm to determine whether or not it should be dispatched to a human.")

Taking the Guest's Emotional Temperature in Real Time (and Before They Get on TripAdvisor!)

One promising way to think of a system such as Ivy is as "real-time satisfaction monitoring." (Or, if you prefer, think of it as "pre-TripAdvisor satisfaction monitoring.) Either way, it's a powerful concept. You can think of it as having a sensor attached to every single guest that blinks red every time there's a bad experience—so you know the right way to take care of it. It's a lot less spooky for a hotelier this way. Previously, that in-room experience was pretty opaque. You know everyone's in their rooms, but you don't know how they're feeling; you end up waiting 'til checkout to ask for the guest's feedback—and the response rate you receive is in the dismal, 2–3 percent range. (And by the time a staffer reviews this feedback, the guest is gone and may be publicly sharing their experience on social media.)

A system like Ivy, on the other hand, is designed to give hoteliers ten times as much feedback, and get it to them a whole lot earlier: a hotel will get feedback from 30 percent of their guests in as little as twenty minutes after check-in. So if the guest encountered dirty sheets, Ivy can alert staff in real-time and give you a better chance of ensuring that every guest leaves with a smile on their face—a long time before they ever get to TripAdvisor and have the chance (and inclination) to skewer you publicly. In fact, Go Moment provided me with data (I have not verified this, so take it for what it's worth) suggesting that Ivy has assisted one of its clients, The Declan Suites San Diego, in rising thirty-five ranks on TripAdvisor—an increase in TripAdvisor visibility similar to what you'd expect from undertaking a multi-million dollar renovation.

THE SECRET OF SUCCESSFUL IN-ROOM TECHNOLOGY: SIMPLICITY

Don't make the mistake of thinking that because guests today are so familiar with technology, it's okay to throw clunky technology with complex interfaces at them and expect patience or understanding as customers struggle to find a workaround. The reality of customers today, especially younger customers, of what they will accept is quite the opposite, because the technology encountered elsewhere in their lives has itself become so much more user-friendly than what previous generations encountered. The relentless focus on simplifying the user interface at Apple, Amazon, Google, and other less visible technology players has set a standard of intuitiveness across the tech industry that customers today, especially Millennials, accept as the norm. As technology and marketing professional J. D. Peterson puts it, "Millennials simply expect technology to work, and to work reliably, with a minimum of complexity"[44] because that's been their experience with the technology that has been at their disposal during their lifetimes.

Therefore, installing complicated in-room remotes, or offering confusing, complex options on in-room thermostats, is exactly the wrong approach here. For climate control, two settings are adequate: + and -. If you install mechanized drapes and shades, they should have at most four settings: open, closed (for the drapes), up, down (for the shades). (And, as far as in-room telephone options, emulate Virgin Hotels in chapter 4 and their single "yes!" button for any kind of service a guest may be looking for.)

The (Increasing) Need for Speed

As I mentioned at the start of this chapter, what your guests expect in terms of speed is growing more extreme every day, accelerating with the pace of technological development. Faster Internet speeds, increased access to the web, the proliferation of smartphones and tablets, intuitive search functions, and always-on GPS are some of the developments that influence the timeliness expectations that customers have. Millennials in particular place a premium on speed and convenience. They're twice as likely as other customers to buy their groceries at convenience stores (in spite of convenience stores' wild markups), and they disproportionately patronize fast-casual options like Panera and Pei Wei, as well as prepackaged to-go food options—all of which allow them to avoid the waiting-around-for-waitstaff routine.[45] But young customers are merely the most visible front for these changes. Customers of all ages now expect speedier service, in part because successful brands, both upstarts and established players, have shown that it's possible to speed up service without sacrificing quality. This new norm creates a risk for any business that fails to keep up with the accelerated timetable that customers demand.

Avoiding the Cliff of Dissatisfaction

One concept to keep in mind as you revamp your operation in the interest of speed is "the cliff of dissatisfaction." This is the point at which a customer loses faith in the timeliness of your company or your product. The length of time it takes a customer to reach the cliff varies from business to business, but it's a risk inherent in every service interaction and business relationship.

A time-aware business needs to actively strive to keep customers safely away from this precipice. Starbucks knows how long an average customer will wait, from acknowledgement ("Can I get something started for you?") to receipt of a finished, customized drink. Starbucks dresses its stores with clever merchandising and appealing decor to make these minutes pass as pleasantly as possible, but it also understands that, ultimately, too long is still not good enough. When "too long" threatens, countermeasures are taken. For example, baristas will venture out from behind the counter and take orders from people who haven't yet reached the counter. Starbucks ultimately lets the cliff of dissatisfaction guide its business expansion. As soon as the company's metrics indicate that the level of demand and the resulting wait times are routinely threatening customer satisfaction, Starbucks opens another store down the block.

Casino management is a highly scientific discipline that leaves the gambling solely to its customers. The team at Caesars Entertainment knows how long the average gambler will wait for a complimentary drink on the casino floor before he gets fed up. They know within how many minutes after arrival a casino guest needs to be greeted before he'll wander elsewhere, as well as how many minutes can elapse between subsequent service touches and free drinks without him moving on. Caesars doesn't rely on intuition to guide how it staffs the casino floors; it turns to staff tracking and other data for help, including the RFID tags I first mention in chapter 2 that allow them to scan the waitstaff's entry and exit of the bar area. This allows managers to track the time a server takes to sweep her section and return to the bar for her customers' orders, data that the casino uses to improve its decisions about staffing and flow.

Want to Outfox Your Competitors? Compress Time

Two hospitals with Midwestern origins, Mayo Clinic and Cleveland Clinic, have become world famous for their innovative approaches to health care. Both hospitals have succeeded in part by challenging the traditional (read *slow*) model of medicine. At the Mayo Clinic, patients fly in from all over the world for "efficient, time-compressed care that can usually provide a definitive diagnosis and sometimes initial treatment, including major surgery, within three to five days," as [46] Leonard L. Berry and Kent D. Seltman, authors of *Management Lessons from Cleveland Clinic*, put it.

Mayo refuses to settle for the sluggish, unreliable timeline common in hospitals today. Just one way that Mayo sets itself apart is in its approach to reading scans, such as mammograms. Less time-sensitive hospitals put all scans, whether taken early in the day or late in the afternoon, into a slowly filling holding "basket," then wait until the evening to analyze and interpret them. This means a patient may be called a day later and asked to suffer through a redo (and another torturous round of waiting) if a technical issue arises with the initial scan. Compare this to the procedure at Mayo, where scans are read more or less on the spot, allowing them to be verified while doctors are still at the patient's side.[47]

Ohio-based Cleveland Clinic's own focus on timeliness has helped it improve its overall reputation for patient sensitivity. By working to match or even exceed the scheduling expectations of its patients, it has improved its patient satisfaction scores from among the lowest 10 percent of the nation to now rank among the world's highest.

Cleveland Clinic achieved this remarkable transformation by working backward, setting "unrealistic" speed goals and then getting to work figuring out how they could be achieved. For example, they had this gutsy goal: They decided that anybody calling the Cleveland Clinic for an appointment (with any complaint and for any specialty) would be seen that same day. Cleveland Clinic's success in pulling this off is quite an accomplishment when you consider it in contrast to the month-long waits some specialists demand their patients endure.

You can test this yourself, if you're so inclined. Call Cleveland Clinic on the phone today and you'll hear a mind-blowing greeting: "Thank you for calling Cleveland Clinic. Would you like to be seen today?" Only after 4:00 p.m. does the greeting roll over to "Would you like to be seen tomorrow?"

Pulling off the same-day appointment feat has been far from easy. The effort at Cleveland Clinic had to clear some high hurdles. Dr. James Merlino, who headed Patient Experience for Cleveland Clinic at the time, says that an extraordinary amount of time and effort are devoted to "managing the flow and ensuring we have the capacity."

This commitment to speed comes in part from Cleveland Clinic's awareness of the growing number of millennial patients it sees and whom it expects to see more of as they age and start families of their own. As Dr. Merlino told me, "Nobody of any age wants to wait, but we understand that the expectations of the millennial generation are especially accelerated, and this has certainly affected our thinking."

Fifteen-Minute Room Service

Not long ago, a Four Seasons property in Boston came up with, and successfully rolled out, hotel-wide fifteen-minute room service. The standard prior, and throughout the industry still, is a thirty to forty-minute wait. In Four Seasons' way of thinking, the prospect of such long wait times was essentially making a significant cohort of today's time-sensitive guests not even consider room service as a viable dining option. "Room service, generally speaking, is not something you think of as being quick," Christopher Hunsberger from Four Seasons told me. "But millennials and business travelers in general want 'quick,' and we realized that the industry's traditional conception of how long is acceptable for a room service delivery time was losing us business."

The Boston Four Seasons came up with the idea, piloted it, and subsequently shared it with corporate headquarters, who have rolled it out at other properties as well. "While it's a simple idea in theory, it's not simple to execute; it requires multiple stakeholders in the organization to coordinate. At the property level, you're talking about the kitchen and room service staff being able to coordinate that and make it happen." But it has been worth it. The new fifteen-minute delivery promise has revamped and rejuvenated the concept of room service and made it attractive to today's guests.

"AND YOUR POINT IS?"

Key Points from Chapter 9: How the Digital Revolution Has Changed Your Customers

▶ Customers expect every business in every industry to achieve "digital parity." You need to be able to offer all the advantages, and be as easy to do business with, as the best of what your customer has encountered online and in self-service solutions.

▶ Interactions should be intuitive, efficient, and fast, and shouldn't require unwanted, extraneous human intervention by either the customer or your employees.

▶ Your processes should provide your customers with control over their own account details, including the ability to modify their service preferences. You, the service provider, should have cross-channel access to this information as well.

▶ Time should be speedy and malleable, like it is online.

▶ These changes in expectations are most completely realized in the newest generation of guests, the digitally native millennial generation. But change has also come to their elders, customers who aren't millennials but have been influenced by a millennial outlook.

▶ Consider the "Jetsons Test" for deciding which service tasks should be off-loaded to automation vs what service should be delivered by humans. If a human can do the job more efficiently or effectively than a machine can, then a human should be doing it. If a person can do the job more *warmly* than a machine, assign that task as well to a person. Otherwise, leave it to the machines.

▶ Improving automated customer service is no excuse to offer lousy human-powered service. Instead, take the resources recouped through digitization and focus them on meaningful human interactions in the places where they count.

▶ Technology, including in-room technology, websites, apps, etc., should be simple and easy to use. Don't make the mistake of thinking that because guests today are familiar with using technology, it's okay to throw clunky, complex technology at them and expect customers to patiently struggle to find a workaround.

▶ Hospitality guests—along with customers in all industries—are increasing their demands for speedy service. Anything you can do to improve your speed of service and/or the extent to which your service matches the timetables of your guests will be appreciated.

Afterword

Farewell for Now, and Happy Hospitality!

W e've covered at lot of ground here, and I hope you've enjoyed and benefited from the time you've spent reading my book.

One way to ensure you retain this material for your day-to-day use is to review each of the "And Your Point Is?" summaries at the end of the chapters whenever you need a refresher.

You can reach me directly to discuss applying these insights more specifically to your situation at micah@micahsolomon.com or (484)343-5881. I wish you happiness in your hospitality endeavors!

Notes

1. Various parts of this BUBL explanation are drawn from Leonardo Inghilleri and Micah. Solomon, *Exceptional Service, Exceptional Profit: The Secrets of Building a Five-Star Customer Service Organization* (AMACOM Books, 2010).

2. From the J.D. Power 2015 North America Hotel Guest Satisfaction Index Study[SM] http://www.jdpower.com/press-releases/2015-north-america-hotel-guest-satisfaction-index-study.

3. I've finessed one detail in this story to protect the privacy of a hospitality professional.

4. The essence of the sequence described is true, but I've altered some of the surrounding circumstances.

5. Leonardo Inghilleri and Micah Solomon, *Exceptional Service, Exceptional Profit: The Secrets of Building a Five-Star Customer Service Organization,* pp 46–47.

6. Portions of the "ARFFD" discussion that follow are quoted from or paraphrased from Leonardo Inghilleri and Micah Solomon, *Exceptional Service, Exceptional Profit: The Secrets of Building a Five-Star Customer Service Organization*, pp. 28-34.

7. *Exceptional Service, Exceptional Profit: The Secrets of Building a Five-Star Customer Service Organization.*

8. Ibid.

9. "Potentially career-ending" is a quote from a physician speaking to author Leonard L. Berry in his book, *Management Lessons from Mayo Clinic*, which inspired this paragraph.

10. Excerpted and modified slightly from Micah Solomon, *High-Tech, High-Touch Customer Service* (AMACOM Books, 2012) pp. 88–89.

11. List and descriptions are from my interviews and correspondence with Danny Meyer and his organization, Union Square Hospitality Group.

12. Susan Reilly Salgado, a managing partner of one of Danny Meyer's companies, shares this in her online article "8 Ways to Hire Great Employees," http://www.inc.com/susan-salgado/8-ways-to-hire-for-hospitality.html.

13. *How Cool Brands Stay Hot,* Joeri Van Den Bergh and Mattias Behrer (Kogan Page Publishers, 2013), p. 41.

14. Ibid., p. 44.

15. The concierge deserves recognition. She is Daisy Undercuffler.

16. Tonya's last name is redacted at her manager's request.

17. (For continuity, these paragraphs have been lightly edited from what Mr. Sharp told me in a more back-and-forth format during our conversation).

18. In collaboration with coauthor Leonardo Inghilleri.

19. Ibid.

20. Details have been changed to protect identities.

21. Seth Godin, "Just saying it doesn't make it true," (blog post), July 2005, http://sethgodin.typepad.com/all_marketers_are_liars/2005/07/

22. Thanks to Mark Harmon of Auberge Resorts for helping me to clarify this.

23. Thanks to Jay Coldren, EDITION Hotels vice president, for these observations.

24. Ibid.

25. I picked up this expanded usage of the term from Seth Godin; he discusses it in his *Seth's Blog* blog post from April 25, 2015.

26. Leonard L. Berry and Kent D. Seltman, *Management Lessons from Mayo Clinic,* 2008.

27. Ibid.

28. *Boston Consulting Group:* "Millennial Passions." (Whitepaper), November, 2012.

29. "American Millennials: Deciphering the Enigma Generation" (Whitepaper), September 10, 2011.

30. Martha C. White, "Free Hotel Wi-Fi Is Increasingly on Travelers' Must-Have List," *New York Times,* July 6, 2015.

31. Boston Consulting Group: *The Digital Road to Earning Travelers' Trust.* (Whitepaper), February 5, 2013.

32. Christine Barton, Julia Haywood, Pranay Jhunjhunwala, and Vikrant Bhatia, "BCG Perspectives: Traveling with Millennials." (Whitepaper), Boston Consulting Group, March 18, 2013.

33. Ibid.

34. "The New Kinship Economy: From Travel Experiences to Travel Relationships" The Futures Company, as commissioned by Intercontinental Hotel Group, 2013 (Whitepaper).

35. Candice Choi, "In Instagram Age, Chili's Pays for Buns with Photo Appeal." (Associated Press, May 14, 2015).

36. David Sax, *The Tastemakers: Why We're Crazy for Cupcakes but Fed Up with Fondue* (Public Affairs, 2014), especially pp 261–262.

37. "The New Kinship Economy."

38. Vanessa Hua, "Asian Americans More Likely to Have Multigenerational Households." (on-line article) Published by NBCNews.com, August 25, 2014.

39. *Management Lessons from Mayo Clinic.*

40. "Shared Experiences Are Amplified," Erica J. Boothby, Margaret S. Clark, and John A. Bargh (research article), published on-line in *Psychological Science*, October 1, 2014.

41. "The Ring of Time," *Essays of E.B. White*. (Harper & Row, 1997) p. 148.

42. Inspired in part by "The New Kinship Economy."

43. Quoted in J.D. Power, "North America Guest Satisfaction Index Study Results, executive summary."

44. Quoted in Micah Solomon, *Your Customer Is the Star: How To Make Millennials, Boomers and Everyone Else Love Your Business* (Rain Dog Publishing, 2015) p. 5.

45. *"Millennial Passions."*

46. *Management Lessons from Mayo Clinic.*

47. Ibid.

List of Hospitality Leaders Who Were Interviewed by the Author for This Book

I'm grateful to the following hospitality professionals and organizations for the interviews that I conducted for this book, which informed and inspired this manuscript. Titles and organizational affiliations are listed as was accurate at the time of their interviews.

Hotel and Resort Professionals

THE ANT STREET INN

Suzy Hankins, Proprietor, telephone interview, July 14, 2015

AUBERGE RESORTS

Mark Harmon, CEO, telephone interview September 12, 2013, as well as a variety of follow-ups by email

THE BROADMOOR

Steve Bartolin, Chairman, telephone interview, February 25, 2015

Ann Alba, Resident Manager, on-site and telephone interviews, August 24-30 and December 4, 2014

Calvin Banks, Director of Training: telephone interview, December 4, 2014

EDITION HOTELS

Jay Coldren, Vice President, EDITION Hotels: multiple telephone, email, and in-person interviews

THE FOSTER HARRIS HOUSE

Diane MacPherson, Proprietor, telephone interview, August 18, 2015

FOUR SEASONS HOTELS AND RESORTS

Isadore Sharp, Founder and Chairman, telephone interview, April 13, 2015

Christopher Hunsberger, Executive Vice President for global products and innovation, telephone interview, December 13, 2013

Andreas Rippel, Chef (Chief) Concierge, Four Seasons Hotel, San Francisco, on-site and telephone interviews, Feb. 15 and March 3, 2016

FRHI (FAIRMONT, RAFFLES, AND SWISSOTEL)

Jennifer Fox, President, Fairmont Hotels, email interview, August 28, 2013

Jennifer Meszoly, Regional Director of Sales and Marketing, Fairmont Southampton (Bermuda), on-site interview March 29, 2013 and additional follow-up by email

Doug Carr, Executive vice president, Distribution, in-person, videoconference, and email interviews and contributions. Doug was also one of the editorial readers of the manuscript.

HYATT HOTELS CORPORATION

Mark Hoplamazian, President and CEO, telephone interview, April 23,

Sara Kearney, who is now Senior Vice President, Operations, Asia Pacific, telephone interview December 16, 2013, as well as various follow-ups via email.

JOIE DE VIVRE HOTELS

Seth McDaniels, Assistant General Manager, The Epiphany Hotel, on-site discussion, April 25, 2016

Jazz Buchla, Front Desk Supervisor, The Epiphany Hotel, on-site interview, April 25, 2016

MONTAGE RESORTS

Craig Schoninger, Director of Sales and Marketing, The Inn at Palmetto Bluff, on-site interview, March 3, 2015

Christine Wrobel, Public Relations and Marketing Manager, The Inn at Palmetto Bluff, on-site interview, March 3, 2015

David Smiley, Director of Guest Services, The Inn at Palmetto Bluff, on-site interactions, March 3, 2015

OXFORD INNS AND SUITES
Robin Baney, COO, email interview, August 18, 2015

THE RITZ-CARLTON HOTEL COMPANY
Herve Humler, President and COO, telephone interview, March 19, 2015

Diana Oreck, VP of The Ritz-Carlton Leadership Center telephone interviews, March 6-7, 2015

Lisa Holladay, VP for Global Brand Marketing, telephone interview, March 6, 2015

Liam Doyle, GM, The Ritz-Carlton Dove Mountain, on-site interview, January 2, 2015

Max Zanardi, GM, The Ritz-Carlton Istanbul, on-site interview, April 2, 2015

3HOSPITALITY
Rupesh Patel, President and CEO; (Mr. Patel is also CEO of SmartGuests. com), email interview, April 12, 2015

VIRGIN HOTELS
Raul Leal, CEO, on-site interview, April 17, 2015

Clio Knowles, VP of People, on-site interview, April 17, 2015

OTHER HOTEL PROFESSIONALS:
Bill Quiseng, hospitality professional and customer service thought leader, email interviews on various dates. Bill was also one of the editorial readers of the manuscript.

Tim Miller, hospitality and customer service professional, telephone interview, October 1, 2013

Food Service Professionals

CRAFTED HOSPITALITY
Tom Colicchio, Chef/Owner, telephone interview, April 14, 2016

EASTERN STANDARD KITCHEN & DRINKS

Garrett Harker, Proprietor, email interview, April 6, 2015

FRONT BURNER BRANDS

Bob Johnston, CEO, telephone interview, August 1, 2015

THE INN AT LITTLE WASHINGTON

Patrick O'Connell, Proprietor and Chef, telephone interview, February 23, 2015, as well as a variety of email interactions

JARDINIÈRE, THE COMMISSARY, ET AL.

Traci Des Jardins, Chef/Owner, telephone interview April 28, 2016

LE BERNARDIN

Eric Ripert, Executive Chef, telephone interview, April 29, 2016

LDV HOSPITALITY

John Meadow, Founder, email interview, May 21, 2015

Noé Alarcon, Wine Director at Scarpetta in Las Vegas (an LDV Hospitality restaurant), in-person discussion, March 8, 2016

SELANNE STEAK TAVERN

Leo Fenn III, Director of Operations, in-person discussion April 3, 2016, with email followup, April 19, 2016

STARR RESTAURANTS

Stephen Starr, Owner, email interview, March 28, 2015

UNION SQUARE HOSPITALITY GROUP

Danny Meyer, President and CEO, telephone interview, March 11, 2015

Theme Parks

SIX FLAGS ENTERTAINMENT CORP.
Jim Reid-Anderson, CEO, email interview, February 17, 2014, as well as in-person conversations with Mr. Anderson and the Six Flags leadership team.

Gaming Industry

MOHEGAN SUN POCONO
Glenn Lawless, Director of Guest Relations, telephone interview, February 27, 2015 (not quoted in book but Glenn's interview informs portions of it)

Healthcare

CLEVELAND CLINIC
James Merlino, M.D., Chief Experience Officer, Telephone interview, February 7, 2014

Hospitality Design, Hospitality Furnishings, Customer Experience Design, Human Resources for Hospitality

ANDREW JENSEN CONSULTANCY
Andrew Jensen, Principal, email interview, August 1, 2013

IDEO
Fred Dust, Partner, telephone interview, December 17, 2013

MAYA ROMANOFF COMPANY
Laura Romanoff, Senior Vice President, Sales and Marketing, (a.k.a. my awesome cousin), videoconference, October 4, 2013, as well as various in-person and email discussions

THE ROCKWELL GROUP
David Rockwell, Founder and President, email interview, October 28, 2013

HUMANeX
Brad Black, President and CEO, telephone interviews September 9 and 16 and November 22, 2013

GO MOMENT
Raj Singh, CEO, telephone interview November 12, 2015

Contributors not listed above:

Bill Gladstone, Waterside Productions, author's agent extraordinaire
Marla Markman, book development expert
The team at SelectBooks
My family, my friends, my colleagues, and my clients

Index

About the Author

MICAH SOLOMON is one of the world's leading authorities on customer service, the customer experience, consumer trends, hospitality, and company culture. He is a consultant, keynote speaker, trainer, and training designer specializing in these subjects, as well as being a best-selling author. His books have been translated into more than a half-dozen languages and are the recipients of multiple awards. Micah is a regular contributor to Forbes.com on the subjects of customer service and hospitality, and his expertise has been featured in *Inc.* Magazine, *Bloomberg BusinessWeek*, ABC, CBS, NBC, and the *Harvard Business Review*.

A business leader and entrepreneur himself, Micah built his own company into a market leader in the manufacturing and independent entertainment field, and he was also an early investor in the technology behind Apple's Siri.

He would love to hear from you at micah@micahsolomon.com, (484) 343-5881, or via his website, www.micahsolomon.com